Submissive Men

Being a Submissive Man In The Modern World

Alexandra Morris

Table of Contents

Introduction

Gender roles are constantly changing and this affects not only sexuality in society but gender roles generally are dictated by the labor needs of any civilization. One of the best ways of illustrating this, perhaps, would be a woman's role in the 1940s and '50s, which changed radically and quickly to accommodate the financial and resource requirements of the economy. When men were called to arms to fight in World War II - indeed, in any war - it was women who had to fill in the gaps in the labor market back home, which could necessitate them working in factories and assembling bombs and weapons, for instance.

In the 1950s, after men had returned from the war and had gone back into the labor market, women became surplus to requirements within the labor force and were encouraged instead to stay at home and raise their families. This was reinforced by governments. Even academic research, such as Bowlby's Attachment Theory, seemed to aim at convincing women that their place was in the home looking after the children so that children could form strong attachments to their primary career; their mother of course. This threw the onus of being the breadwinner heavily back onto the male who became the dominant member in the household and who could expect his house to be cleaned, his children to be cared for and a hot meal waiting for him and served up by a wife who had done her best to look pretty for his return. Women were pushed out of the labor force and told to know their place.

This shift in roles can be clearly observed and is well documented in advertising campaigns showing the woman having clearly defined menial tasks and the man adopting the dominant role and leaving the home to do important work. Advertising on the new-fangled television and in magazines demonstrated how deliriously happy women were to have vacuum cleaners and washing machines and soap powders that removed all stains. Even fashion reflected a nipped in waist and dirndl skirts emphasized those lovely child bearing hips and the feminine form of a woman who would appeal to the men she lived to serve.

This quite clearly pervaded into the sexual arena. In the United Kingdom, for instance, there was a commonly used phrase, "Lie back and think of England," intimating that only the man took pleasure from sex and a woman was just doing 'her duty' and wanted to get the actual act over with as soon as possible. Because so many lives had been lost in the war, and men had been absent for long periods, the 1950s produced the generation who later were to become known as the *baby boomers* that enjoyed advantages that had been denied to their predecessors. As more domestic appliances became available, life for women became easier and so men expected them to be looking attractive and for them to be sexually available on demand.

There cannot be anything new under the sun in a sexual sense. Everything is cyclical and even pedophilia, although largely prohibited and regarded as taboo worldwide now, has at times throughout history been acceptable almost across the globe. Indeed, it is still part of normal society currently in certain parts of the third world and this is precipitated by that society's economic needs. There are huge expanses of women who are never exposed to any formal education and their role is still to look after the menial side of family life.

Women have been the submissive part of a couple for centuries and in an effort to prove a woman's purity practices can be extremely brutal and barbaric. Currently there is no thought or effort put into providing an education for huge swathes of women in third world countries. Their lives are simple and any opportunity to break free from that lifestyle is severely limited. In thirty countries in Africa, Asia and the Middle East, UNICEF estimated that in 2016 there were 200 million women who had been subjected to female genital mutilation (FMG). This is the horrific practice of removing the external parts of female genitalia with a blade and normally occurs within a few days after birth and often before the child is five years old. It occurs mainly in countries, which are Muslim and is performed for cultural, sexual and modesty and purity reasons. The clitoris is often cut away denying sexual gratification for the woman and the vagina is sewn up, leaving a small hole for urination and menstruation. When the man has sex with the girl for the first time he forces himself into the woman. It is mostly done by women who regard it as a great honor and who believe that their daughters and granddaughters must receive this mutilation to escape social exclusion. Needless to say, this causes many health problems and there are no health benefits. There is now international condemnation of this practice. It is hardly surprising that the pendulum is beginning to swing and that women would want to escape from these harsh treatments.

In the 1960s, with the advent of the contraceptive pill for women, roles began to change in the Western world at least. Being in control of when, and even if, to have children, freed women up to enter the labor market themselves. Education became a much more viable option and an increasing number of women were able to enter the upper echelons of commerce and industry, albeit at a lesser salary. Indeed, this financial anomaly still exists today and has quite recently been a hot topic of debate in the western world. Women became independent and realized that they did not actually *need* a man to support them because they were quite capable of doing this for themselves. There have been many countries across the world now that has had a female political leader. While the United Kingdom has had two recently, America came close with an almost-ran, Hillary Clinton.

And still, the emasculation of the male population continues. The contraceptive pill helped to mark the 1960s as *The Swinging Sixties* where anything went and the female population could engage in free sex - sleeping with anyone she wanted but still gaining the title of slag and slut and any other derogatory banter that might be shared in the golf club, where women were often still not allowed (Gentlemen Only, Ladies Forbidden). Women who were already in the workforce were used to sexual harassment and often a little tap on the backside as they passed someone's desk only earned the offender a title of office "letch." At the very worst, he became a joke amongst the women and a bit of a lad amongst the men. Women's emancipation was all a bit of a joke really because women had always been regarded as common property of the male population to be whistled at in the street and touched up near the photocopier. More recently, there has been an absolute uproar in America and the United Kingdom about male sexual harassment, much of it historical and dating back decades. Harvey Weinstein is perhaps the most famous to be named and shamed and even Donald Trump did not escape condemnation for his pussy grabbing antics but remarkably still went onto become the President of America. So it wasn't really all that serious.

While the earth continues to shift beneath our feet, so too does sexuality and it wasn't until 2003 that the legal rights of LGBT people were recognized in America. Indeed, all levels of sexuality seem to be infiltrating into the modern world sexual arena as minority groups demand recognition of their human rights and are encompassed within the whole. Recognizing our individual feelings and inclinations and making sense of them can be equally daunting and leave us with a sense of feeling abnormal and unsure of how to satisfy needs that may largely be viewed as distasteful or just plain kinky by the larger society.

There are so many factors and influences that make an individual what they are. Each of us is unique and because the topic of male submission has not been openly and freely embraced by society – yet - it can be difficult understanding feelings that do not seem to fit into the mold. This book helps to help answer those questions and should help you realize that if it feels right and does not hurt anyone then just do it. After reading this book, I hope you feel set free to be exactly who you are sexually and realize that enacting fantasies can be enormously liberating and hugely enjoyable.

Chapter One – What is Normal?

When we think of being submissive generally we are more likely to think of women, rather than men but as the world constantly changes, so too does sexuality for both genders. Fifty Shades of Grey has addressed through the medium of pop culture what it means to be a female submissive. And even though ardent feminists are probably vehemently in opposition of the portrayal of women being exploited for cheap thrills on the screen, it does address a part of sexuality that really does need more exposure (forgive the pun).

If we try to define 'normal' there are many more than fifty shades of it. Our sexual preferences are, to a degree, biological but they are also governed by every experience, sexual or otherwise, we have been exposed to throughout our lives. We might try hard to fit the expected norm but an internal struggle can start and if left unexplored can fester and cause psychological problems. Discussion and openness of sexual preferences should be welcomed so that the degrees of normalcy can be identified and accepted by a wider society, not denigrated by ignorance and fear: your own or others'.

It can be exceptionally difficult sometimes to determine what governs your sexual inclinations. The reasons behind sexual preferences and practices are complex and you may not even be aware yourself of what has formed them within your psyche. If laws are introduced to protect society, then we should question more minutely the determinants of those laws as an individual and as a society.

For instance, let us ask why homosexuality should be outlawed? Was it perhaps to protect the traditional format of a family to produce children and maintain a cohesive civilization? Tax laws were introduced to promulgate a traditional family, which in turn was expected to lead to a cohesive law-abiding and financially stable society. And historically, we were all so thoroughly indoctrinated to agree that homosexual practice was abhorrent and a sin against mankind. We are now suffering from overpopulation so there seems to be little requirement for homosexuals to be arrested and locked up for their crime and the law is being relaxed. While homophobia is still very much alive and kicking, more people are at least opening up to its place in a modern society and prosecution is lessening.

However, imagine how much damage that maltreatment has already caused. And that has been achieved by keeping the masses under control and angry at the perceived cause of their deprived plight so that the queers amongst us could be regarded as pariahs. On an individual basis a homosexual, or indeed anyone who does not fit the accepted prescription, could be damaged long term and grow old thinking he or she is perverted and weird. How sad is it to realize that so many people have fallen beyond the realms of happiness because they did not accurately fit into shape that the present economic climate demanded?

The point that should be made here is that homosexuals are not hurting anyone and that there is no reason for them to be persecuted. Prejudice on the grounds of sexuality is as baseless as racial prejudice and no coherent and intelligent argument could be used in its favor. More often than not it is not a conscious decision to be who we are sexually. Our preferences grow with us, but we can be made to feel as if we are outside of societal norms and we desist from doing what we really want or hide it and deny it. As educated as we become about any subject, environmental influences can have a huge bearing on what we internalize and how we come to view ourselves. Can it be reasonably accepted that as long as we are not hurting anyone, we should be free to fulfill our sexual desires with any other consulting adult?

Of course, there will always be those who say that anything other than traditional sexual intercourse, without any kind of perverse behavior, between a man and a woman is wrong. By *traditional* let us assume that means one man and one woman using the missionary position. How boring and unappealing would that be? It can be of no surprise that people who always adopt this position have a special night of the week for it and it is never spontaneous. Repression of natural desires is unhealthy, irrelevant and not required in a society where a happy sex life contributes to a healthy mental and emotional state.

And, on the subject of health, being with a submissive male partner, women are much less likely to suffer from male violence. A survey entitled *the National Crime Victimization Survey* conducted in 2006 and included rapes and sexual assaults that were *not* reported to the police said that 232,960 women reported suffered such crimes, which is more than 600 a day. Another disturbing figure is that there are around 120 million women worldwide who have either been raped or forced to participate in some other sexual act. The perpetrators are most often husbands and boyfriends or former partners. Another startling statistic is that 74% of humans trafficked globally are women and children and nearly 75% of these women and children are used for sexual human trafficking. I could go on but I think these statistics very starkly prove a point that women are still being exploited and used as sexual objects by people who no longer regard them as human. Submissive males begin to sound like a very safe and healthy option for everyone concerned, not least of all for society as a whole.

Equally, wanting to participate in the behavior of a submissive male is only a single facet of sexual normalcy. Each individual has multiple predilections towards myriad behaviors, which can easily change and be dependent on a factor as trivial as mood. We should be grateful that we have freedom of choice, which allows us to be who we truly are and embrace it.

Being a submissive male does not have to be hardwired and a regular practice or one-dimensional. It may be something you experiment with and decide to adopt at varying levels in different circumstances and times. At first, it might seem unnatural. You may have been fighting against it all your life up until that first brave moment you decide to relax and enjoy yourself. Even during the act, you might hear that voice inside your head telling you that what you are doing is wrong. Or, conversely, you might regret not having tried it before and wasting time and feeling at once that this is an experience that you are going to embrace and accept into your life on a regular basis.

It's unfortunate that many of us suffer from inhibitions that have no sound basis in fact or commonsense, and yet they are instilled into us and stop us from leading a healthy and fulfilling sex life. It's almost as if that thought has been introduced in much the same way as a habit is learned. You are exposed to the concept over and over again, sometimes consciously but mostly it is insidious and you do not even realize how your opinions are being carved out inside your head. But then an inclination that is at odds with your trained and ingrained thoughts and beliefs is introduced and this is where the conflict can start. For you to be reading this book suggests that you might be at this stage.

But remember, habits can be broken. And that is done by practice and by the acquisition of knowledge and the breaking down of solid barriers to your happiness. This book seeks to provide the answers you might have been looking for and most of them will already be within you. It is about exploring who you are and how you got there. But mostly, it's about who you want to be and how to achieve that, specifically being a submissive male, both sexually and generally.

Of course, there are many professional "Dommes" out there who are very good at what they do and you may choose to experiment with one or more of them. Or you may want to do it within the boundaries of a close relationship where adopting the role of a sexually submissive male adds new and layered dimensions to explore and enjoy, a role that you may like to flip at times and instead become the dominant. Within these pages, we will look at the many elements involved in being a submissive male and how to get the best out of your experience. Hopefully, by the end of it, you will have a greater understanding of why you personally feel its importance to you and how to achieve your objective of enjoying the role to its fullest.

Chapter Two – Who Am I?

There has been much research about from where our sexual desire emanates. Is it nature or nurture? The answer seems to be a mixture of both.

The consensus is that some sexual arousal is partly innate and utilizes two structures within the brain, namely the amygdala and the hypothalamus. This is the part we are born with and occurs instinctively and without our being aware of its operation. This is called 'cued interest'.

The other part, 'un-cued interest' is developed through early experiences and is at its strongest when we are developing sexually and erotic thoughts prevail. These are obviously going to be much more variable than the cued interests because we are all subjected to widely different experiences and so ultimately we have no control over what turns us on sexually.

It might be something so obvious as being spanked as a child and that corresponded to having erotic thoughts, which continued into adulthood. No doubt that spanking was given by someone who made you feel safe and whom you trusted to show you what was right and wrong.

Also controlled by our brains is the instinct to be either dominant or submissive, or even both, as the circumstances dictate, and both are hardwired into our brains to give us sexual gratification. The expression of, 'expressing his feminine side' may be truer than we first thought on the face of it. We can compare this to the animal kingdom where we see female dogs mounting other females or male dogs mounting other males. The roles can become blurred and interchangeable and produce sexual stimulation.

The biological part in the brain seems to be much easier to explain than its partner. There have been incidences where babies have been born as one gender but for one reason or another have been raised as the opposite sex. Even though the child has not been informed of the circumstances, they have still reverted to the original gender role. One such famous case is that of David Reimer in 1965 who when undergoing circumcision accidentally lost his penis. His horrified parents consulted a famous sexologist Dr. John Money who convinced them that if they operated on the baby and gave him a vagina instead he could be successfully raised as a female. They did this and he was injected with hormones that made him grow breasts and develop womanly curves.

Despite his parents' best efforts however, he rejected everything that was considered to be feminine and instead displayed masculine behavior and traits. No longer able to keep up the charade, when the child reached the age of 14, his parents told *Brenda* that actually he had been born *David*. He was hugely relieved and went on to undergo further operations, which gave him back a penis, although it was non-functioning. He also had a double mastectomy to remove his breasts and eventually even went on to get married. Sadly, at the age of 38 he committed suicide by shooting himself through the head because he was unable to overcome the very successful brainwashing that had been applied throughout his childhood. This clearly indicates that fighting what comes naturally is not a healthy way to deal with sexual inclinations that are regarded as being unwholesome by the general public. The enforced denial of natural instincts in fact is totally unnatural, and an ill-conceived way of attempting to shape everyone to the replicated model of a preferred prototype of the majority.

In a study carried out by Ogi Ogas and Sai Gaddam's *A Billion Wicked Thoughts. What the World's Largest Experiment Reveals about Human Desire (2011)*, they posited that men were turned on by visual representations and women were turned on by romance and stories. For women, sex was more cerebral. This study was done using the Internet so that it allowed people to complete a survey on their sexual preferences allowing them to be completely frank, but this study diverged from previous ones by its anonymity. For that reason, it was regarded as being more honest and probably more accurate than its predecessors. This research validated the assumption that a man is ruled by what's between his legs and it also proved that men have more sexual neural pathways to the brain than women have. As soon as men are presented with visual erotica they are aroused both physically and psychologically. Incidentally, it also came as a surprise to discover that men are more aroused at the sight of an erect penis than women are.

This male one-track mind must be tempered with an explanation that they are wired to view women as vehicles that can be used to propagate the next generation. To ensure this, it is reasonable to suppose that is why man is not essentially monogamous, and so it is an understandable instinct to have developed evolutionally in their brain. Men have neurologically developed to be dominant whereas women are conditioned to instinctively search for a partner who can provide safety and security for herself and her children. Or so it has been historically but now that is perhaps due for redesign to fit in with the Earth's needs.

The report also shows that men are turned on by what they consider to be new and novel, which might explain why they seek new experiences which could sometimes be perceived as being outside the norm, such as being a submissive perhaps. Playing the role of sub opens up a whole new avenue for exploration. This could be a prolonged chapter or a brief interlude but new territory often is more appealing that a path well-trodden and predictable.

Another cue for arousal is a sense of danger and this could be evoked by a sense of difference and because male submission is regarded as taboo by many still in society. This might be because there is a feeling of doing something, which is socially or culturally, regarded as forbidden, perverse and not acceptable by the masses. Just by performing the taboo task alters the physiology by quickening the heart rate, raising the muscular blood flow and making us breathe faster. This is controlled by the sympathetic nervous system, which is also responsible for, surprise, orgasm. This no doubt accounts for the part that fantasies play in our sex lives. Imagining ourselves in perilous situations at which we are at the mercy of someone else can help us to climax. So that would seem to suggest that actually taking part in a physical role play, playing out that fantasy, must be so much more powerful and add enormously to sexual excitement and arousal.

If you confide in a potential sexual partner or close friend and they think you are weird or abnormal, turn that back on them. They are unable to break out of their conditioned harness and are tied down with their own guilt about having a traditional sexual role and unable to break out of it or even think beyond its realms. You are the lucky one because you have given the matter much intellectual thought and should now be fully aware of what excites you and how to get it. Each to his own, and it is probably accurate that you are having a better time than the ones who have settled into a comfortable corner and never dared to move out from it. Leave them with the saying "*Don't knock it until you've tried it!*" And don't give them a second thought. You are on an exciting journey while they dare not even take the first step towards fulfillment.

Relinquishing responsibility to someone else can also be a very effective way of escaping from the normal stresses of life. By passing over the reins to a dominant and submitting to their desires offers release - in more than one sense of the word. It can be a place of safety where the sub becomes helpless and needs the dom to take care of him, reminding him of the safe haven he felt as a child.

There are many physiological reasons for men to wish to adopt the submissive role and this does not just apply to sex, as we'll explore in another chapter. The suggestions given here are not exhaustive but probably some of the most common. These feelings can develop at any stage in life and should never be regarded as being abnormal as long as they hurt no one else.

Matriarchal or matrilineal societies still exist in some parts of the world. In Greek mythology, the legendary Amazon tribe existed entirely of women. They were warriors whose prime concern was war and this tribe was sexualized by many *Carry On* type films. However, societies ruled by women still do exist and they have no doubt evolved out of the need of the land where they were born. They adopted practices that would ensure their continued existence. For instance, in many of these matrilineal societies land and property passes down through the woman. The Mosuo in China is probably the most famous with around 40000 members. Property and lineage are passed down through the woman and the man stays with his own mother. They do not have a word for husband or father and simply go from man to man without marrying. They invite the man to have sex with them or just go to his house to have sex and then move onto the next one when they feel like it. Fathers of the children rarely know who their father is and there is no stigma surrounding this. And amongst many others, lineage also passes through the woman in Judaism. Compare this to our own western society and we start to get an idea of how easily we are controlled to answer the needs of the land.

Perhaps it is not unreasonable to imagine that the physiology of our brains evolves just as other parts of our bodies do over long periods of time. As external influences shape the type of human we need on this planet, hopefully our thought processes will work to control how that is achieved, as well as working the other way too. Sadly, this process normally takes eons to occur. However, if our neural pathways can be built and destroyed by any number of methods, including chemicals and alcohol, then surely it is not too incredible to believe that this is actually possible. Indeed, we may even discover a faster route of achieving any desired outcome. So not only will it be influenced by physical changes within the body, namely the brain, but also by environmental factors exerted upon it. As our knowledge about the human brain grows, so too does our capacity to make changes (improvements?) within it.

Finally, something that we all are capable of controlling immediately is the way we think. It would be unfair to be judgmental of others' sexual inclinations, regarded as perversions by someone on the outside looking in. If you are already a submissive man, thus going against the constraints that the narrow mindedness in a modern western society places upon you, then you should be aware of how punishing opinion can be against your own sexual inclinations. Try to understand others and let them do their own thing. The more open and permissive we all learn to be about sex the easier it is for everyone to lead a healthy and fulfilled life, which is multidimensional. Keep your mind and your heart open and be willing to share your wisdom. Only you know how long it took to acquire it. Let us move out from behind the closed doors and closets where suppression and self-doubt can only lead to unhappiness. I am not professing you take out an ad declaring your sexual inclinations because I think more than one person might find you a nice padded cell. But rid yourself of the feelings of guilt and realize that it is not wrong to want to live out your fantasies; it is instead wrong to deny yourself or anyone else that opportunity.

If it feels good, do it!

Chapter Three - Submissive to Alpha

Being a submissive man does not mean that you have to be submissive in all areas of your life of course. The degrees of submission are on a sliding scale and cover a very wide spectrum. Many men choose to keep it just to the bedroom while for others it may be integrated seamlessly into their day to day household activities. The roles of submissive and alpha are also interchangeable and even during a sex session an individual can flip from one to the other. It's about what the couple feel comfortable with and desire.

Even the heads of multi-million dollar organizations or top politicians may need respite from the daily grind of constantly being in control and having to make decisions that can potentially affect others' lives fundamentally. It cuts across social class and the reasons for have submissive tendencies are remarkably complex.

It might be a surgeon who literally is responsible for making life or death decisions on a daily basis. It is understandable that high powered males who are required to exude an unmistakable air of authority and be the alpha male in their working lives should need to relinquish that responsibility from time to time and escape a very demanding reality. This does not mean that they do not enjoy their profession; in fact, it may mean the very reverse, that they give everything to it and it is emotionally and mentally draining. And relinquishing control to someone that they love and trust is far healthier than resorting to drugs or drink. And far safer.

Being a submissive or living out the submissive role playing may happen very infrequently or it may be a planned event with a partner or entail an occasional visit to a professional domme. It may be different every time or it might be variations on a theme. At first, an alpha male may well struggle with swapping roles, even though he craves to do so because he has been so well conditioned throughout his life into believing that he must always be the strong man and be in charge at all times. Incredibly, should a well-known public figure reveal a sexual preference for being a submissive it still may be a cause for public titillation and it is doubtless a sign of denial in many cases for men who are overtly alpha. It takes courage to come out and admit to yourself what your deepest desires are, especially when everything you have been taught up to now is to be the exact opposite of what you want to do. But it doesn't have to take over your life. Not all submissives have dungeons in their basements and a cupboard full of sex toys that would make a nun faint. It's a question of degree and what suits you personally.

Nevertheless, an alpha male may struggle to let the facade of manliness down but it can be done by introducing subtle changes into normal life. For instance, let's take a hypothetical example. An alpha male may well take inordinate pride in being a breadwinner and providing for his family. It is ingrained into him deeply by a family who were traditional and were not fortunate enough to explore any opportunities, educational or otherwise but had to concentrate on acquiring and maintaining a secure and safe environment for their child. Our submissive male, on the other hand, has had the privilege of a good education by the good grace of his parents, and has the luxury to spend time on self-exploration and forming trusting relationships. He knows himself well, including sexually, and has reached the point where he is ready to put into practice some of his fantasies of male submission.

So far, his orthodox upbringing has perhaps held him back but one day, he picks up a magazine or meets someone at a party and this one day changes his life forever. He decides to take note of the new information that has been presented to him and is determined that he will follow the advice to become himself. His workload is so heavy, he is extremely successful in his field and yet he has been yearning to find a way of seeking some respite from the heavy burden his professional life places upon him. And his search begins. It takes him into new circles where he finds that he has no reason for guilt and that he is not the freak he has feared himself to be. The new knowledge and sight of the lifestyle he wants to acquire are evidence of all things being possible and within his reach.

He is already in a stable relationship with a woman he loves and trusts, so how does he begin to integrate his desire for being submissive? It is not only linked to the sexual side of him but he wants to share a burden of responsibility with his partner. So he makes a plan. He earns enough to take hold of the financial reins but one way of introducing submission into his life is to let his female partner be responsible.

This is something that you might like to introduce into your life but it is entirely dependent on your circumstances and preferences. There is actually a name for this and is it "findom." It might be completely or just in certain areas. You might go to a restaurant for a meal and she insists on paying. Slowly, the idea of sometimes being out of control gently infiltrates your lives together. It might be as simple as you might let your partner choose what to watch on TV, even when you want to watch golf, but you subjugate your own needs for hers and even find you enjoy it and even discuss the program afterwards. You ask your partner to make important decisions for you both and agree to do as she decides, always letting her have the final word. You run a bath for her and help her to undress and dress, maybe rubbing her body down with oil afterwards. The important message is that you do what she wants you to do without question because she is in charge and you do as you are told. You are placing your free will, even if only in certain areas, into her hands.

The distinction between alpha and submissive males can appear as being very distinct but it is rare to find a man who is completely one or the other. It can never be that black or white and all human beings are thankfully multidimensional and have many layers that make them into what they are. Historically, it was always thought that women preferred the strong he-man portrayed in pop romantic novels as being able to make every woman in sight swoon with the heady delight of passion as he took her in his muscular arms and ravaged her. A little woman needed someone who could be constantly in charge of everything and make snap decisions on momentous topics.

In parts of the world, in countries that exist around brute strength and which depend on leaders being autocratic to get what they want, an alpha male leader must be domineering and command respect, earned or not but probably the latter. But studies done by Cheng et al (2010) on university athletes showed that the alpha males within the group were found to have unlikeable characteristics such as being unethical and immoral, narcissistic and generally disagreeable. They were described as not being cooperative or helpful, were not all that popular and in fact were low on self-esteem. By contrast, their prestigious fellow beta members of the team were the ones who took the role of leader and they in turn were described as popular, cooperative, helpful and more intelligent and they had better social skills and higher self-esteem.

This is a clear indication that different attributes are required in different circumstances. For instance, if a giant of commerce or industry, who is at the top of his game, was sent to an overcrowded and violent prison, as a prisoner, he would sink to the bottom of the pile in an environment for which he was ill-equipped to deal and he would have to adapt to survive in a hostile and strange place. Attributes that made him popular would help that survival and this transfers over to civilized societies. A leader must listen to those he governs and take their wishes and needs into account. Otherwise, evoking nothing but negative feelings, sooner or later he will be toppled. And the same rule transfers easily into more personal relationships.

In recent decades male and female roles have blurred around the edges and women welcome the softer side of men, especially in a lifetime partnership where both are responsible for major decisions. Ideally, the relationship is so open and trusting that an alpha male can confide his desires to his partner and they can discuss in depth how far they want to go sexually.

Experimentation should be easily facilitated and both partners must feel comfortable with it. Sexual relationships should always be reciprocal, at least to some degree, or there can be little joy for the partner who is getting no gratification from the union.

Sometimes, a submissive male may want to keep this side of his nature apart from his long-term partnership. This might be because he already knows that she would not accept the idea under any circumstances and he does not want to put an otherwise perfect relationship to the test by insisting that she takes on the role of domme in the sexual side of their relationship. Or it could be that doing it secretly adds an extra frisson of danger and magnifies the experience and heights of sexual gratification and pleasure. Everyone's circumstances are different and you must find your own level that makes you feel comfortable and happy, ideally without hurting or deceiving a partner. You know your own circumstances best and no doubt you will consider them carefully before risking everything for what could be classed as 'a bit on the side'. Cheating on a partner should never be acceptable under any moral compass in any kind of relationship. Ask yourself how you would feel if you found out someone was cheating on you behind your back. A later chapter is dedicated to this subject.

Fundamentally, self-awareness is paramount. Should you decide to explore this part of your psyche for the first time and you have always considered yourself to be an alpha male, you should consider why you feel the need to do so. What is it that excites you about this sexual foray? The answers can be extremely illuminating and lead onto enormous leaps of self-knowledge, which can enrich relationships and sexual enjoyment.

Think about two gay men in a relationship and how they may well find role adoption of sub and dom much easier to adopt than a heterosexual couple who have assumed traditional roles. Gay men are used to having to adopt the role of alpha in certain environments, especially in their professional lives but maybe to their families too, even though it may go against the grain. After a while, it should become automatic. After all, we all adopt many different *hats* for different situations - that is we react differently within each group we may belong to, be that work, home, family, social etc. Everyone we know knows a different me.

What you show yourself to be in your professional life need not be the sum total of who you are. It may be part of what attracts a women to you but then, like any other relationship, there has to be different aspects to explore within that relationship. Like any other union between two people, it is about a shared sense of values and an ability to find common crossover points where you can identify and empathize with each other. This is a step on the route of the alpha male sharing his submissive side and it is up to the couple involved how far they want to travel that route. To find out then you must discuss it and find a level that suits you both. You don't have to jump in with both feet; in fact it could be totally terrifying to suddenly produce a set of handcuffs and a whip instead of the normal bunch of flowers you might present your partner with. Talk about it first.

Of course, it's always about balance. Most people will respond to another person who is kind and responsive, interesting and interested. The two roles of alpha and beta can cross over at numerous points and this might be across the professional and personal arenas. Most men - and women - will be a mixture of these two and even if your profession calls for a level of dominance, different facets of your personality can still be introduced alongside to foster a feeling of empathy and cooperation. You are in charge of the role you adopt and that goes for all areas of your life. There is no concrete rigidity of how you adapt along that spectrum. Learn to be confident in your own skin and go for what you want and what makes you and your partner happy. Don't be afraid to show your feminine side either because that soft and gentle persona will always be acceptable by everyone you meet. If it isn't, it's their problem, not yours.

Chapter Four – Foundation of a Healthy Relationship

Let's be real here. Female-led relationships are rare, and this gives both submissive men and dominant women very few resources to refer to. There isn't a formulaic approach to building the perfect FLR. And because it's not as common as its MLR counterpart, this seemingly blurs the lines of boundaries and gives a rather foggy idea of what makes a healthy D/s relationship.

I'm going to dissect this dynamic to explain what I mean. A relationship that is dependent one a party more than the other never lasts. Female-led doesn't mean that women will be the center of your world, where you'll do nothing but serve them and await their appraisal and validation. This is dependence, and it's unhealthy and unattractive to women, which I'll explain in more detail later.

Submissive men do have power in the relationship; it's just channeled in a different manner. You choose to submit, and the moment you opt-out of this dynamic, it stops. There is no (actual) contract that binds you to be a slave or a sex servant. You merely choose to act like one because it turns both you and your partner on. Approaching women with the mindset of filling some sort of void that you have has never ended well. This is never what dominant women seek.

For instance, some men may approach a dom, thinking that the relationship will involve being taken by surprise with sexual acts that may be done anywhere and anytime. And while, in theory, it may sound hot to pretend to resist sexual intimacy, it's not fun in reality. This is why you need to establish boundaries before you start having sex. Consent is the foundation of your relationship.

Boundaries pretty much include everything. Some couples may want to have a D/s relationship inside and outside of the bedroom. For instance, I've met some men who enjoyed it whenever I ordered them to do the housework for me. You'd think they only get off on dirty washing panties, but even being made to do the dishes satisfies them, because it makes them feel like they're useful to their doms beyond the parapet of sex acts.

Other couples may prefer to keep this dynamic in the bedroom and share a conventional relationship otherwise. This all depends on what you and your partner like, and it's not just something you find out as you go with the flow. If you decide to do something against your will thinking that it's part of the package, you'll grow to resent the relationship eventually. And let me assure you that your female partner would be disgusted to know that you're doing something that you don't want to do. Force is not what makes a D/s relationship. The choice to submit is.

On the other hand, boundaries also make sure that both of you equally enjoy sex. Some men may like feet; others find them disgusting. You wouldn't want to be compelled to indulge in a fetish that you don't enjoy, thinking that it's just the way it is. It's not. You and your partner make the rules. You don't blindly follow kinks you see in pornography unless you both decide you enjoy said kinks. Share your fantasies and see what you're both allowed to do.

You see, just because you're the sub in this relationship doesn't mean that you can't set the rules. That's something you need to do before you initiate sex so that both of you feel comfortable, and equally enjoy the experience. This is why I always view D/s relationships as something that can only be gradually built along with trust. I wouldn't advise men to meet a stranger off a dating app and immediately allow them to immobilize them in bed whilst blindfolded. Female-led relationships, especially when it comes to sex, are based on trust. You must trust the person not to cross the line because it can go downhill very quickly if you do.

Another aspect of a dominant-submissive relationship is openness, but that doesn't come without its own set of rules either. Because let's face it, individuals in the BDSM community are far from conventional, and they're always open to trying new games, even if they're not initially sure about them. It might be fun to try them out, but it may also be difficult to opt-out without coming off as pretending to resist, as part of the game. This is where a safe word comes in handy.

A safeword can be anything bizarre that you normally wouldn't say in bed. So I'd avoid anything such as no, or please stop because these can all be deemed part of your power-play in bed. Always use a safe word if you ever feel like you're in too much in pain, or if you otherwise feel uncomfortable for any reason during sex. This gives your partner a cue for a "time-out," and she should stop immediately. Some couples also like to use a green/yellow/red system. This way, you can easily allow you, partner, to proceed (green), take it slow (yellow) or stop (red).

That said, I'd like to stress how establishing boundaries is not just limited to doing so with your partner. I've met many men who weren't realistic about what they expected and what they could actually tolerate. You can easily get off to porn, showing men getting their cocks and balls stepped on because, in theory, it's sexy when you're just lying in bed and thinking about it. In reality, it takes some great tolerance to pain to enjoy such acts. When you tell a dom that you enjoy certain kinks, she will naturally presume that you have tried them, and have thus had experienced pleasure from them.

If there's anything you haven't yet tried, but like the idea of, I'd suggest being open to your partner and asking her to be gentle and work her way up by using the green/yellow/red system to see how far you can take it. If the pain is not pleasurable, never be afraid, to be honest about that. It doesn't make you look "vanilla" to be less tolerant of pain than others. Your mistress wants you to enjoy the pain as much as she enjoys inflicting it, so always be upfront about how you feel during your power-play.

Now that the importance of boundaries is established let's move on to something I'd like to stress on, and that's how some men can be needy and mistake that for submissiveness. Surely, your mistress will enjoy being spoiled and being the center of attention...in the right context. Some men grow an unhealthy obsession about serving women, possibly in a subconscious attempt to fill a void. And while I feel bad for them, let me tell you that dominant woman are certainly not your therapists.

A woman will always tell whether a sub is playing along to the power dynamic, or is genuinely obsessed with being around her and having nothing else to do than pleasing her. And let me tell you that she won't like the latter if she senses it. On the other hand, you should always find a community where people share your interests – as in other submissive men seeking mistresses. You need to teach yourself about what the common power dynamic is like, and what it usually entails. Some men approach sub-dom relationships as though they will have no say in the rules. Or rather, they find it easier to do so, which also stems from being needy.

When you initiate a female-led relationship with such an attitude, you immediately come off as a leech. Surely, it's fun seeing someone who genuinely enjoys serving me, but what is the point if they have no other interests of their own? Needy men have as much personality as a brick wall, and that makes them anything but appealing partners to doms. And aside from what women think, it's not healthy for you to pursue such a relationship for validation because it will simply never work, and only means that you're seeking this power-play for all the wrong reasons.

A submissive man initiating a relationship will always propose a consent checklist, and will usually be the one establishing rules about what he's willing to do and the kinds of punishments he's willing to receive. I've known submissive men who weren't big on humiliation and only liked a little whipping on the side. While other men may be into full-blown humiliation, licking toes and being spat on is only the tip of the iceberg. The bottom line is, if you don't want to come off as a leech, always set some ground rules which show that you know what you like and what you're serious about investing in the relationship.

Another thing you might want to work on is your expectations. In your own fantasy, you think of yourself as a slave to your mistress who provides. You're at home with your male chastity belt and leash on, awaiting the arrival of your dom. Once she's there, you're ready to present your body to her whenever she feels like it. In theory, it sounds like a dream come true, but it's also a rather juvenile way of thinking of female-led relationships, primarily because all the realistic details are forgotten.

You will sometimes get sick. She will sometimes be too exhausted to engage in BDSM play and will go straight to bed. At times, you'll spend a day or two like a conventional couple in a vanilla relationship because one or both of you are sick, tired, or just not in the mood. You're not signing away your soul. You will both still get to choose to opt-out of this dynamic whenever you want to, and that's something I highly advise you to stress on before you start engaging sexually with a dominant woman, especially if you're new to the game.

I always advise men to see their submissive sides of themselves as just that: aside. It's not what makes you; it's not your entire personality. Because when you think of it as who you are, you'll find it increasingly challenging to say no when you don't feel like it. You'll find it impossible to say the safe word even though it's a little too rough for you. And this is all but healthy. You want to be able to tap into character. I understand that submissive men are generally submissive beta males, but that's not what I'm referring to right now.

And that is not to say that power-play only applies to sex. You can still do chores for your dom, and you'd be actively playing along. The point is, whenever you need a break, you're entitled to one. If you find that there is no off button on your power game, then you're in an abusive or a miscommunicated relationship that needs to be fixed or mended.

Now that I've covered everything that could possibly go wrong with FLR let's get to the good part. In my opinion, D/s relationships, in general, are much healthier than their vanilla counterparts. Whether conventional couples realize it or not, the relationship is never equally dependent on both parties in regards to everything. There are always disparities, and there will always be one partner who's more dominant than the other. The difference is, vanilla couples don't incorporate that into their sex lives (as intensely), and they don't really admit the existence of this dynamic.

On the other hand, this is the opposite of how I view FLR in particular. It's an honest expression of who leads, even though both parties fairly contribute to where the relationship goes, and both have control over it. I see this is never successful with vanilla relationships because the power dynamic is not clear, there's always resistance on both ends, and a party usually ends up exerting more effort in the relationship.

When you and your partner have explicitly agreed that you're the sub in the relationship, this allows each of you to know what is expected of you to give and receive in return. Each of you has a role, and each of you exerts equal amounts of effort in the relationship, although you channel it in completely opposite manners.

An FLR is the perfect yin-yang.

That is when the yang likes to get spanked.

In general, I personally find D/s relationships more expressive and much more sensual. Nothing says trust like being tied to a bed blindfolded, unable to anticipate when or where you'll get a whipping next. You trust that your partner will not hurt you, and will only inflict a pleasurable amount of pain. It's exciting. It keeps you on edge, and it's this dirty little secret between you and your partner that no one else knows about.

The idea that people see a completely different person out in the social sphere makes your D/s relationship more special. Only you get the privilege of seeing your partner in full latex with a paddle. And similarly, only she can be intimate with you in such a way. It's sensual and sexy, and it brings couples closer. I think there's something unique about BDSM power play in general that makes couples much more passionate about each other. They tend to grow a spark that lasts because their relationship is always exciting.

I'd also like to reiterate that a healthy D/s relationship can have, according to my own experience and that of others, some mental health benefits. It's hard to come out to people about being submissive, especially when you're a man because they tend to view you differently and associate negative connotations to something that you enjoy in a safe environment. But most importantly, people in vanilla relationships don't realize how D/s couples have it better. You can analyze my sexual tendencies through Freudian theories all you want, but does it matter why I may like these kinks if they're practiced with someone I trust in a consensual manner?

When I talk about healthy D/s relationships, I inevitably have to bring this up. Are they healthy to begin with, even though some may argue they are only sexual tendencies that stem from child abuse? I wouldn't care too much where they come from, as long as you ask yourself these two questions:

1) Is this consensual?

2) Do I feel safe?

If the answer to both of these questions is yes, then go ahead and do whatever you want. Get slapped and spanked, get your torso stepped on by high-heels before your mistress ties you to a cross and whips your ass. You're a man with unconventional kinks, and you like to be humiliated by your partner in an elaborate sex dungeon. It may sound unorthodox to others, but I'll take consensual, safe sex in a heartbeat if it makes both me and my partner happy. So whoever argues that what you share with your partner can't be healthy, shrug it off and put that leash back on. You don't have to confide in others about what you do in the bedroom if it makes you feel uncomfortable. That's another reason why D/s can be exciting. It's usually secretive, and that makes it all the more fun.

Now that you know what makes a D/s relationship healthy let's take a look at how you may want to incorporate power-play in your everyday life. As I said, some men may enjoy being dominated in the bedroom, while others would be interested in making a lifestyle out of it. I'm going to be demonstrating the latter. Men who seek this kind of relationship can refer to themselves as 24/7 submissives. A fair warning, though; it's not for everyone.

There are oftentimes rules that are made about the kind of clothing you can wear at home. Some women may demand that you wear chastity belts, others may ban boxer briefs or any kind of underwear. You might be required to wear a leash or a full body suit on some days, depending on the rules that you set together beforehand.

When I say that you'll be a 24/7 submissive, it's much more flexible than it sounds. That means that you still have time for work and housework, and you usually incorporate this kind of play in your common free time. For instance, you may be required to put on such outfits as soon as you come back from work. That doesn't mean that you need to prepare yourself for sex daily, because you'll find that it's a little unrealistic for long-term relationships.

Many mistresses also like to tease men. You may be spanked on some nights, teased on others, and you may spend a week or more without intercourse, only edging. It's sexy and makes intercourse much more fun, as it feels like a reward that you've earned. Sex takes time and investment, so teasing is a much sexier way of delaying sex than flopping yourself on the bed and promising your partner that you'll try to be less exhausted tomorrow.

That's another thing I respect about D/s relationships. You schedule everything and set realistic expectations.

Today you get a whipping. Tomorrow, I'll sit on his face while I have a cigarette or two, and on the weekend, I allow him to penetrate me, but only if I'm on top. It's all organized and planned, and it's always different. Sometimes, I may surprise him with a reward that he doesn't expect, and his reaction turns me on. This is what you'll be in for when you date a mistress, and it's equally exhilarating and healthy for both of you.

Generally speaking, if it doesn't feel right, then it probably isn't. What I love about BDSM is how animalistic it is – how it satiates our deepest instincts in the wildest ways possible. Your gut feeling is equally important when you engage in such power-play. If there's anything that makes you feel uncomfortable, always be open about it. Use a safe word or the green/yellow/red system I mentioned above. You'll know that you're in a healthy D/s relationship, and you'll easily see red flags when there are any. Loosen up, and get yourself that mistress.

Chapter Five - It's Not All about Sex

Submission does not just apply to sex of course. A man may choose to be submissive in other ways. Below is a list of suggestions. It's not exhaustive and I'm sure that you could think of many more.

Financial

We touched on financial submission in the previous chapter. This is when a submissive man chooses to let his partner take care of the finances. Whatever he earns may go straight into her bank account or maybe a joint account but he might be given an allowance or has to ask for anything he needs. There are practical and organizational advantages to this as well as emotional. If one person is in charge of the purse strings then all expenses and outgoings should be centralized and under control. This would send out a clear message to the woman in the relationship that her submissive partner trusts her to take care of the important things that matter in their lives such as keeping the roof over their heads and ensuring all the utility bills are paid and not in danger of being cut off. This would be the case especially if he is the only earner in the home. She can become the lady of leisure who lunches while he goes out to work to keep her in the way to which she's become accustomed.

This is a very different scenario to the 1950s when women were 'the little woman at home'. By the 1960s, the bra burning had begun and women fought hard for their equality. What might have been a better goal to aim for would have been supremacy. Because they were not only fighting for the freedom of being able to work and decide when and if to give birth but also for equality in the workplace. For many of them, this meant joining men in the labor force again, at a much lower pay rate, and running a home too. Hardly equality. Even though things are slowly catching up now as far as the spread and share of domesticity and childcare is concerned, there is still a long way to go.

Findom does not have to be as clear cut as the male submissive asking for money as and when he needs it but it can be beneficial in such a way that the couple has to discuss major purchases before one of them goes off at a tangent and spends large amounts without consulting the other. Even by pooling the resources of both earners in a couple, if one person holds the strings then there will be no nasty surprises in store for the other partner and this method should encourage excellent financial literacy in a couple and an organized pattern of regular spending. This does not, of course, mean that common sense has to go out of the window and give license to the female to spend, spend, spend on things only for herself and neglecting essential household bills. So do check in from time to time, just to make sure you have a partner who is totally trustworthy and knows what she's doing.

Housework

It is now becoming more and more common that a man is in charge of the housework rather than it being the sole traditional role for women. Indeed, it might well be that he is the better cook or better at cleaning than his partner. He may enjoy shopping and looking for bargains or treats for them both. This would fit in particularly well when the woman is a full time worker and the man does not work or works only part-time but nevertheless, this doesn't necessarily have to be the case and there doesn't have to be a reason. Quite often, this kind of regimen will occur naturally and evolves over time. Other times it might be agreed by a couple and last for varying amounts of time as decided upon by both parties. This can be on a scale of always making the meals or becoming a domestic slave. So it could range from being sent on errands to being a total domestic slave. Parties within a relationship might agree to swap traditional roles so that a man might do all the household chores and the woman does things like decorating and car maintenance. Sometimes it can be a natural preference and other times it can be an agreed - or enforced - decision between two people.

Parenting and Childcare

For a couple of decades now it is increasingly common to see a man who is responsible for full time childcare. As more and more women enter the professions and their earnings outstrip those of the man, it makes more financial sense for the lower wage earner to stay at home with the children full time while the woman goes out to work and supports the family. This might be because they have decided that the child needs a full-time parent at home to look after them and be responsible for raising them. Or, it could be that the cost of childcare is prohibitive. No doubt this fairly modern trend will have a knock-on effect in line with the way modern economies develop: it could affect how children develop. Alternatively, being responsible for children's welfare and wellbeing full time may alter how the caregiver perceives himself on a more global scale.

Objectifying

This is acting as an inanimate object and serves as a form of humiliation. It might be a piece of furniture for instance so that the male is on all fours and the female rests her feet on his back while she drinks wine and watches TV. Jeff Gord, a bondage artist, called this forniphilia and specifically describes the act of human bodies being incorporated into pieces of furniture. Gord used to extend it to is nth degree and make people part of the furniture so that they would have to stay immobile for long periods. Often they would be gagged and there would be a danger of suffocation so that the submissive's welfare had to be checked regularly. This does not have necessarily lead to sex but could certainly be a method of foreplay and certainly humiliation.

Foot Worship

This is similar to objectifying but the submissive male would lie on the floor and the domme would rest her foot on his face for long periods. It is common for the

Domme to wear stiletto heels in this scenario, which she may use to press into his face or other parts of his body, including his genitals. He could also be told to go on all fours and be made to lick her boots or suck her toes and feet.

Golden Rain

This is allowing your partner to urinate on you and again is a method of humiliation. It can be done onto bare skin or through see through tables so that the urine doesn't have to touch the skin. Some men perceive this act as an honor rather than degradation because the act is so intimate and they are allowed to be part of it.

Acting as a Human Ashtray

Not to the point of stubbing out the cigarette on them, depending on taste I suppose, but as another form of humiliation. A sub might kneel in front of his mistress with his tongue out for instance and she flicks her ash onto it.

Feminization/Sissification

This is when the submissive man dresses up as a woman and acts in a feminine way to appear like a woman or even an exaggerated version of a woman. Going out in public might cause more humiliation - or the sub might enjoy it more! This might go as far as wearing a wig and makeup and dressing in a particularly vulnerable female fashion such as schoolgirl or even in a maid's outfit so that he appears subservient. The man's name may change into its feminine form so Tom becomes Tomasina or George becomes Georgina. He may be given names such as princess or baby or more derogatory names such as slut or whore. Giving relevant chores to the persona make may it all the more humiliating; perhaps they have to answer the door to the postman like this.

Trampling

This is the act of literally walking over someone in an attempt to cause him or her pain or at the very least humiliation. It is most effective when the dom wears stilettos of course.

Verbal Abuse

This might be about the size of the penis or how stupid he is. It is about attacking the ego not destroying his self-worth. It's about stripping back the ego and reducing him to an obedient servant to the woman's will and desires. It should be carried out authoritatively and with confidence so it reaches its full impact and is realistic. Women can enjoy total dominance over their male partners but this does not necessarily mean that they have to be cruel all the time. A man must earn a woman's favor.

Subjugation of Ego

This explanation almost goes without saying because a male submissive wants his needs to be secondary to his partner's. This might be as simple as letting her choose where to eat out or who to see socially, whether he likes them or not. If he doesn't behave appropriately he would be punished for bad behavior. By doing this, the male appears tender and the female should not be afraid that she is being selfish because she is doing what her partner wants her to do. This type of behavior is common to all areas of life which the couple share and should be practiced at all times until it becomes second nature.

Primarily, a submissive man is seeking the loving approbation of a significant female in his life and if she takes control it might stem back to a dominant female from his childhood who was always in charge, but he didn't mind because he always felt safe and loved by that person. Conversely, the dominant woman from his past may never have found him good enough and so he must constantly strive to improve to impress the significant female figure in his life. The dominant female partner takes the place of that significant woman from his past and makes him feel cherished within the boundaries of domination.

Renting Him Out

This is a good way of earning a little extra money. The woman asks friends if they have any non-sexual jobs they want doing such as gardening, decorating - things that her partner can easily manage in his spare time. However, any money he earns has to be paid directly to the female and a private report given about his work. Freebies could also be offered.

Again, this list is not exhaustive. The objective of the exercise is to ensure that the submissive male hands over any authority of part of it to his partner. This can be in just one area or as many as you can think of. It is primarily about suppression of the male ego and allowing the female to take charge of situations. Try and be creative. Opportunities to exploit this form of non-sexual domination abound in everyday life and it can prove enormously liberating for both parties.

Chapter Six - How to Find Your Dominant Woman

Statistically, submissive men seeking dominant women far outnumber dominant women seeking men to dominate. However, that is not to say it is impossible; in fact, far from it. And there are various way of achieving this.

Personal Ads

The most obvious would seem to be placing your own personal ad but you should be extremely cautious and use a new email address. Your ad should be as appealing as you can possibly make it because you need to attract as many potential partners as possible. You should know what sort of a person you are looking for so that they can identify with what you want, but more importantly you should clearly state what you could offer them. Like any other relationship the other person needs to know if you have anything in common to start with so at least you have something to build on and are not going to be sitting like two dummies when you get together.

When you have exchanged sufficient emails to make you feel comfortable ask for personal details and exchange more photographs. Perhaps you could then progress to chatting online. There are so many ways to do this and I am sure you already have a preference but Messenger and What'sApp are free and you can get to know each other very well through this medium.

Finally arrange to meet but always in a public place for at least two to three dates. Some might argue that meeting someone from the internet is dangerous rather than in a natural situation in real life, but is it really any more risky than meeting someone you have only met once in a social situation or whom you see at work and whom you know nothing about? If you didn't take any risks, then you'd never meet anyone. Just use your head and be sensible. Take things slowly and get to know each other. Be sure you can trust each other and, if meeting for the first time, then leave a trail so that in the event of anything untoward happening, you can easily be tracked down. Have someone call you after a certain amount of time to check that you're okay and have a code to specify that you are - or not. If not, then make your excuses using the call as the reason why you have to leave so soon.

After discussing general things such as work and hobbies, try and discuss in detail what each of you want from the relationship. Is this likely to be a long-term, loving relationship or is it all about sex? Should it be monogamous or are you both free to have other partners? When you have proven yourself to her she may be ready to take it onto the next level but never try and force things. That would not be appropriate behavior for a submissive. If you have started off by placing an ad focusing on a submissive relationship, then bringing up the topic after chatting for a while about more general things is not untoward. Rely on your instincts and you should know when the time is right to bring the subject of sex up. If she seems uncomfortable, then perhaps you have chosen the wrong moment or have been too premature. On the other hand, if you have been specific about what you are looking for, there should be no problem about at least asking how she feels about it in principle. If she backs off completely in horror, then ask if she has had second thoughts and no hard feelings felt.

However, there can be problems using personal ads in that you are using your desire to seek a D&S relationship as your prime focus and motivation instead of meeting someone and building a relationship first, after which you introduce the other sexual elements. In that way, the trust should already be present and you are practicing in a loving and safe environment. On the other hand then, if you are simply looking for someone to share your enjoyment of this sort of sexual titillation, personal ads may be an acceptable way to meet someone and you're both clear from the start that is all you are after. Use it as a way to practice and experiment. At the very least, it can be a pleasant social situation when you can practice your submissive social skills.

Try and let the woman take the lead after you have discussed what you want. If she is experienced, then take this as an excellent opportunity to learn and feel your way along the path to submission. If she is a novice, then you are both learning together and should discuss ground rules and how you will both feel safe. Discussing what you want in detail can be erotic in and of itself.

Make sure that she is aware of any pain boundaries you do not wish to cross; this might need some experimentation so let her know that it is going too far by agreeing on a safe word so she knows she has to be more gentle or stop altogether. The safe word you use should be something that is not part of normal daily conversation such as *giraffe* or *banjo,* something totally obscure. If you simply make the safe word *stop* your partner will not know if you really mean it or not and may have to stop what she is doing to ask you, which could spoil the moment. You will find your own level of tolerance but this does not deter you from trying to please her in other ways. You should be treating your woman like a queen. Listen to her and take note of what she wants and what she needs you to do for her. Do not overstep the boundaries agreed. Every relationship finds its own level and that includes every relationship you are likely to form.

Leave a Calling Card

If the person you want to be with is in your workplace, or perhaps somewhere else you go regularly where there are a lot of people, it might be an idea to test the water before plunging in. It could be part of the game to make it fun. You could have anonymous cards printed which intimate that you are interested in finding a domme and ask that person to leave a relevant sign to indicate if they are interested in getting together. Make sure your cards looks classy rather than tacky. The sign that they leave to show that the feeling is mutual could be a soft toy wearing a blindfold for instance. In fact, there are dominatrix bears readily available on the Internet. If you go in next day and there is a blindfolded teddy on everybody's desk then you know your game is a bit of an office joke so at least you know that the answer is probably no. If, on the other hand, the teddy is on the desk of that special person you could move in and ask that person out.

If the woman is sexually adventurous or up for trying new opportunities at least, she will at least be curious about who has left the card. When you declare yourself, it is up to her to say yes or no. Start by inviting her out for a drink or something else equally innocuous. The woman can tell any curious people who asks what the teddy bear is doing on her desk that she was given the bear by a boyfriend or husband as a joke because he thinks she is a slave driver. While you're out, drop into the conversation that it was you who left the card or that you liked the blindfold on the teddy. You should play it by ear but don't rush at things with all flags flying. Get to know each other a bit better first and then enjoy each other.

Look Out for the Right Woman

This may sound obvious but if you are looking for a domme then you should not be asking out the shy and timid wallflower, however nice she is, at least not when you're just starting out. This sort of partner might be for when you are much more experienced and for that time when you are confident enough you can teach her to be who you want and need. Let's face it, some women are never going to be comfortable playing the domme and you don't want to mar your submissive sexual journey by having the memory of an hysterically upset female trying to escape you.

Look out for assertive and confident women, aggressive even, someone who already feels comfortable about bossing men about. Ask her out and go from there. If she is already dominant, she will most likely be able to tell instinctively that you are subservient and start enjoying taking full advantage of it. Open doors for her, bring her flowers, and treat her like a princess. The relationship should develop naturally when you let her have her own way constantly and always demur to her wishes. Of course, don't let anyone totally trample all over your feelings. You still have needs of your own and although you might enjoy role play and demur to your partner's wishes some of the time, you still should command respect and love. Who wants a fantastic sexual if it is with someone who holds you in genuinely fierce contempt? Relationships should be built on trust and love and even acts of punishment should be meted out with the welfare of the recipient uppermost in the domme's mind. It is about giving you what you want, not necessarily what you deserve. Although of course, these two might well be the same.

Join a D&S Support Group

Most major cities have these now so you are already starting off in the right place to find someone of a like mind by being a member of such a group. Be prepared to be one of a large and eager queue of men, which outnumbers hugely the number of female dommes who are likely to be part of the group. This ratio is probably representative of the numbers to be found generally so it may well be difficult to meet your special woman. There is also likely to be female submissives there as well as transgenders, plus any other kind of sexual oriented individuals or couples but at least in an environment like this the odds of you finding the right partner are lowered. Try and appear confident and as if you know what you're doing. If the right woman is there for you, she will find you and many happy times will lie ahead.

BDSM or Fetish Clubs

Although these might be regarded as some as being sleazy or tacky, most are far from it. Even if you don't meet *the* one, they are lots of fun and you should bump into lots of interesting and colorful people looking for a great night out. Dress for the part so that you get into role and get ready for an eye-popping, lip smacking night where anything goes. Obviously, there's going to be people of all persuasions here so the more you dress like a submissive the easier it will be for you to attract the right sort of person. Be aware though, your submissive outfit might also attract a lot of attention from gay men so have your answers ready for any unwelcome invitations. And by that, I don't mean that you have to be rude. Most people who attend these sorts of clubs are there for a good time. There will be novices and old timers.

Usually, there is a game room in a fetish club where you will be able to see people attached to all sorts of equipment and receiving their punishing. People don't usually mind if you watch or why would they be there in the first place? If you get lucky, they might even ask you to join in. At the very least, you are likely to have the time of your life. There is also usually a bar and a dance floor. Just be careful whom you leave with and make sure someone knows about it. Have your wits about you and be very clear about what you want. You don't want to be found floating down the river the next day with a plastic bag on your head! Not that this happens as far as I am aware (joke!).

When you have made a fair few new contacts, you might be able to narrow them down into a group of only submissive men and dominant women. You could invite them to a party either at your own place or hire somewhere out and charge admission. Tell everyone to dress up in appropriate clothes. Perhaps you could ask someone to provide entertainment by being strapped down and used for pleasure or just maybe a male strip show. It's your party.

Visit a Professional Domme

If you can afford it, treat yourself to a session - or two - with a professional domme. This is an excellent way of experimenting with what you want and you are literally learning from an expert so it would be money well spent. If your first experience is not up to your expectations, don't be put off. Make sure that you ask her to fully explain what is likely to happen before actually doing it. Ask her about the full range of services on offer and if any appeal to you then you can ask to try them out. You can also experiment with your threshold of pain level. The first one might not be right for you so move on to someone else. No-one's feelings can be hurt when you are paying for a service and you are paying for not just satisfaction but a lesson too. Think of it as finding an instructor, like you would for any other thing you needed to learn: driving, playing a guitar. Sometimes, it matters very much who your teacher is. But at the very least, it's a good night out and probably one you will never forget!

Home Grow Your Own

This is probably the best method. Find a woman with whom you are compatible and build the trust before introducing your submissive desires. You could start showing your submissive side in a non-sexual way to start with by offering to make dinner or fetching coffee or putting her feet up to rest. The ways to give your partner a treat are boundless. When she starts to demand that you do things for her, open up and say that you want to try something a little different because you like her being in charge and that you want to cater to her every whim. Learning as a couple can be fun but she might just surprise you by taking to her new role as domme like a duck to water.

You could try taking her to a fetish club if she's up for it. This would certainly spice up your sex life and you only have to take part in the things you choose to. It might give her and you some ideas though. Of course, it might be that your partner is already sexually adventurous within your partnership and that things have become rather predictable. Introducing voyeurism into the relationship can certainly heat things up. Going somewhere like this is a good way of gaining new inspiration. Get her to put you on a lead and make you go down on all fours when you get there. Maybe you could have your drink served to you in a bowl and have to lap it up at her feet. Maybe you could dress very appropriately as well.

Internet Dating

Look out for specific sites out there and get to know someone online first. Preferably, you want to find someone close to home because even though you can conduct an S&D relationship long distance, it is so much more difficult. If you can't find one you like, then you could always start your own. You could do this on social media sites. There are lots already on Facebook for instance and if it's yours, it can be geographically sited. You're free to make the rules then of what can and can't go and you get to screen everyone who wants to be part of the group so you also get first pick.

Get Out There!

Widen your chances of meeting someone. You'll never meet anyone sitting on your couch, watching TV and just wishing. The more people you meet, the better the chances of you meeting someone who fits the bill. Join night classes where women are likely to be in abundance or exercise classes like Zumba or whatever the flavor of the moment happens to be. Learn something that will come in useful in your new role such as massage. Be friendly in public places, friendly not weird, but there's no harm in smiling and wishing someone 'Good morning'. There might just be an instant attraction that makes you click.

* * *

Finding the dominant woman of your dreams is a little challenging without a dating app or website. The rapid growth of the BDSM community has made it possible for individuals to find the right match for them through designated apps like Fetlife and KinkD. And while these services can make your life easier, they rarely ever tell you how to successfully set up a profile that attracts the right partners.

I've personally come across many dating profiles that immediately turn me off, some of which just try too hard to explain the obvious in simple terms that could have been a little cleverer. Coming across a profile with a bio that says nothing but "Looking for a sexy woman to dominate me" makes me immediately look elsewhere. You're on a Fetish app; you don't need to state the obvious. So without further ado, let me cut to the chase about how you can set up an attractive online profile in a way that makes you stand out.

Mystery

No one likes walls of texts in the bio section. You need to leave a little to talk about with your future mistress. The sexiest part of a healthy sub-dom relationship is building it up; getting to know your dom as you slowly establish a bond. If there's anything I encounter more often than not, it's men who tell rather than show in their bios. "I'm a funny man who knows how to make a woman happy."

Let *me* be the judge of that.

If you want to come off as someone with a good sense of humor, make your bio funny. Impress me by writing something clever and catchy; and at the same time, something that actually says something about your personality rather than what you enjoy. Surely, these dating websites are basically a gateway for fun casual sex, for the most part. But that doesn't mean that dominant women want to get straight to it. They'll want to get to know you, see if you click, before they decide they're going to annihilate you in bed. Or in their mini sex dungeon.

Photos

My least favorite part of dating profiles is when they use stock images of submissive men, or photos of handcuffed wrists. Stock photos aren't going to get you anyone, so always upload photos of yourself.

While sexy photos can be fun, you don't necessarily have to upload a picture of yourself in bondage to appeal to women. In fact, if it's a casual photograph, which leaves plenty to the imagination, that usually makes it more intriguing and a little more mysterious. Finding someone who suits you should never be stressful and doesn't require a professional photoshoot of you tied to a canopy bed. Be and look natural, and women will likely pick up on your submissive tendencies just fine.

Oversexualization

You're on a kink dating website, which is already sexualized enough. Even the most dominant women want to save themselves the hassle of running into creepy men who only see them as sex objects. That said, most of us wouldn't care if you upload photos of yourself butt-naked as long as your bio isn't overly vulgar, no matter what your intentions are with potential matches. Either upload casual photos with a kinky bio, or the other way around.

Don't let your profile make you look like you're a premium user on a porn website.

If you want to include something sexual that you enjoy doing, tuck it in somewhere in an otherwise decent paragraph. It's random, it's cute, and it makes you seem more empathetic and less of a sex addict.

Self-Centered Bios

This goes for both your bio and your interaction with any woman you meet on a dating app. Dominant women aren't tools for your pleasure. An FLR is a mutual bond, where each party contributes to pleasuring the other. Don't inundate your profile with things that you enjoy being done to you, because that will make you come off as a man who's only seeking his own pleasure.

Doms will order you to eat them out, suck on their toes, and fuck them; and if you don't appear like you'd enjoy that, then what's the point? While I've initially advised you to avoid making it about yourself, I would also add that you keep it simple and subtle. Don't give off too much information about what you like, and leave some space for you and your potential match to converse.

Research

Porn mostly caters to men, so if your knowledge in sex is based on what you've seen in adult films, then it's all based on male pleasure. Women in those films may seem to enjoy doing nothing but slapping cocks and teasing balls, but in real life, women like to get something in return as well. Look up forums that cater to women; see what dominant women enjoy and what kind of pleasure they like receiving.

That's what you should include in your bio and in your interaction with your matches. A woman who expresses interest in you will go out of her way to ask you what you enjoy, so you don't need to make your kinks the center of the interaction.

To sum this up, let's demonstrate what an unattractive profile looks like. Below is what would turn women away:

- Stock photos/No Photo
- Extremely long bio
- Self-centered bio; for example, "I enjoy being whipped and having my balls tied."
- Overly suggestive bio; for example, "Here for hookups. Let's meet up and fuck!"

On the other hand, here's what dom women would likely look for:

- Multiple photos of yourself
- A clever bio that shows some personality other than just sex drive.
- A bio that makes it about women; for example, "I'll do whatever you tell me and accept punishment when I fail to do so."
- Some room for mystery in the bio

I suppose there is no right and wrong way to set up a profile, just an ineffective and more effective way to do it. By following these tips, you're much more likely to make matches. I'd also advise you to target fetish apps and stay away from generic dating apps like Tinder or OK Cupid, because you're less likely to meet doms there.

Chapter Seven - Communicating Your Needs

Adopting the lifestyle of a submissive man does not have to be all or nothing. It is all a question of balance and if you are in an excellent relationship but where you cannot entirely embrace this role, you have to ask yourself if being a submissive is worth jeopardizing an otherwise perfectly ideal relationship. It's something you should know definitely before putting everything on the line. But you should also know: it is not all or nothing and there can be compromise so that both parties get what they want and are happy providing there is sufficient communication.

If you are lucky enough to be in a happy and established relationship, it is probable that you are already conversant with your partner's sexual desires and proclivities. But after a while, most sexual relationships settle into a pattern and without stepping outside of the habits you have formed as a couple, sex can become boring and predictable, something just to get through for the woman especially. Being a submissive man does not have to dominate your life (hah! wordplay!). No one wants to share his or her lives with a complete doormat so it is important that you find a level and work this out between you. Having an exciting and adventurous sex life will take you down many paths if you allow it to. Being a sub might be just one of those adventures.

Thankfully, we have been given the gift of speech and so this should, in theory, make it easy for us to express to our partner what we want. But despite that many still struggle to open up and simply lay it on the line. If you find talking about it naturally difficult, it might be a good idea to write down questions that you want to give your partner the answers to. I have set out below a suggested list of questions, which you could print off and hand over to your partner at a prescribed time. Feel free to add any of your own because there is no one who knows you better than you, hopefully! It also includes suggested gestures, which can be used associatively with your partner asking the questions and your psychological processing of the answers alongside. This should be done when you are both fully relaxed and feel comfortable and in a place where a sex session could easily be the culmination, that is on a couch or bed.

You are about to open up and tell her your deepest desires but it will be done using a process of questioning and your answers should be as lengthy and informative as you can make them. Do not be afraid of showing emotion. Laying yourself open can be a deeply moving experience for both of you. Showing her a side of you that she wasn't aware of can bring you even closer together. You are doing this exercise to explain to her at length why this type of sex excites you and so that she fully understands how that instinct has evolved within you. Firstly, you should be naked. Ask your partner to dress in a dominant and sexy outfit and find a comfortable place, resting your head in her lap. Tell her not to reprimand or challenge you if she hears anything that she doesn't like or agree with; that can be tackled later and punishment meted out as required. The object of this exercise is so that you can convey to her how and why you are feeling like you do. It might be a good idea to read the first part of the chapter to her so that she can ask you any questions of her own about the process before you begin on the questions proper.

This is only a suggested list. Something to get you started. Add or subtract those you feel inappropriate to your life's story.

1. When was your first orgasm?
2. How old were you?
3. What made you climax?
4. Who were you with? Describe them.
5. Was your mother responsible for your discipline?
6. Did she ever spank you?
7. How did you feel about it when it happened?
8. Was she ever over-dominant?
9. How did that make you feel?
10. Did you have sisters?
11. Were they dominant towards you?
12. What about other females in your life? Were they dominant toward you?
    a) Grandmother
    b) Aunt
    c) Teacher
    d) Nanny
13. Have you had a lot of girlfriends?

    Why have you had so many/few?

14. What sort of woman attracts you? Is she demure or raunchy?

15. Why do you prefer that sort of woman?

16. Describe in detail your first sexual experience?

17. Was it a good experience and if so what did you like about it?

18. Was she dominant at all? Or did you have to take the lead?

19. How did you feel about that?

20. What sort of thing excites you most?

21. Tell me about your fantasies in detail. Which is your favorite?

22. Why does that excite you?

23. Do you have any fetishes?

24. Would you like me to wear leather/lace/PVC?

25. What would you like me to do to you?

26. Have you ever told anyone that you want to be dominated by a woman?

27. Did you ever get to that stage with a woman?

28. If so, how did it feel?

29. If I want to dominate you, will you let me do it totally and submit to me entirely?

30. Would you like to experience pain our sessions? If so, describe it. To what level?

31. In what areas of your life are you willing to submit? Sexually? Financially? Totally?

32. Would you like me to spank you or whip you?

33. Do you want to be publicly humiliated?

34. Do you want me to verbally abuse you?

35. Do you want to be forbidden to orgasm? Totally?

36. If you trust me, tell me your deepest secrets, the things you have never told anyone else before.

37. When do you want us to start doing this?

38. What would your favorite sex toys be?

39. What would you like to wear for these sessions?

40. What would you like me to wear for these sessions?

No doubt you will answer, "Straight away," and you can get started instantly. Remind her before you start that she should start off in the dominant mode, squeezing your balls or stroking your penis but then when she is asking more probing questions to soften up so that you feel safe opening up to her. You might feel that some of these questions do not apply to you and are not relevant but each suggested question reveals something important about you to your partner.

Perhaps she could write a list of questions for you too so that information is a two-way road. And so is the reciprocal pleasure.

This exercise is as revealing as you both want it to be. However, I would suggest that if you feel safe you are as honest as possible. There is no point lying about how you feel or you are taking a step backwards rather than towards what you want. She might deviate from the questions if you should say something that she does not fully understand and that is fine as long as you come back to the list and keep on track. Agree before starting on the questions that if either of you feel uncomfortable it is okay to stop but that you must give a reason for you doing so. Otherwise, the exercise will create more problems that it alleviates. This is about enlightenment and sharing so only honesty is allowed. Saying that, try not to be brutal and say something that is so hurtful you will never be able to retract it or move past it. Hopefully, you know each other well enough at this stage to know that you must treat each other with respect and that your partner's feelings are important to you.

Chapter Eight - Start Slowly

Okay, you've made the decision that you want a dominant female partner and you want to play the role of submissive. You might have analyzed why you feel like this or maybe not. It's not essential that you do but self-awareness is always useful because if you do not know why you feel like this, how will you explain it to any potential dommes? We've discussed how you would find a partner who is in accord with what you want to do but how do you get started, especially if you're both novices?

You might already have ideas going around in your head - and they might have been there for some time already - but now you have bitten the bullet and decided to go for it. Of course, it depends on your circumstances as to where you will start but let us assume for this example that you are starting off from scratch and that you and your partner are learning the ropes, perhaps literally, together. If you're lucky enough to have found a partner who is totally sympatico then you are already streets ahead but for our purposes here we will use a brand new partnership, neither of whom has any sexual knowledge of each other.

So, it's your first date and you have persuaded your lady to come out to dinner with you. You bring her flowers and compliment her on how lovely she looks. Be attentive and open doors and pull out her chair. Let her choose where she wants to go and ask for her opinion about what she thinks you should eat and drink. Make sure that you have taken care of the transport and never interrupt her when she speaks. Always defer to her superior opinion and advice. In short, be subservient and eager to please. You are in the process of setting the scene and preparing the way ahead.

It is a good idea to get to know each other well first if you are looking for a long-term relationship and this is not just about what you are seeking sexually. In this way, you are building trust in each other. It's about finding out what you have in common and if you have the same sense of humor and values. You should be able to assess whether this woman is already a dominant because she will be self-assured and confident, expectant of your chivalrous behavior because she is used to being in charge and getting what she wants. If she seems shy and timid, this does not necessarily mean that the relationship is a non-starter. There is no reason that this person cannot learn to love being dominant but it will probably take more time to get to where you want to be. Take your time and enjoy yourselves and listen to what she has to say.

Over time, you can open up. If she is a skilled communicator you will find yourself telling her things you have never told anyone before. There are people out there who just seem to have a perfect knack of extracting the most intimate information from you and it can be almost cathartic. If she is truly empathetic she might be able to help you towards the path of self-analysis and may even share some of your hypotheses and have ones of her own to share. You are in the process of building a strong relationship, brick by brick so lay a firm foundation.

Gently introduce the topic of your desires to be a submissive and that you are seeking a domme. Talk about the sort of things you like sexually but please choose the right time and place. Unless the sole purpose of your meeting is sex then it might be unwise to introduce this topic in its fullest depth very early in the relationship. You're out for dinner and say, "More wine? And I would like to be tied up during sex." NO! Wouldn't you run a mile too? And she would probably be laughing as she ran. Or screaming.

By the time you do get into more detail, you may or may not have had sex together but it should be getting easier to talk about your sexual preferences. Perhaps you could suggest watching a raunchy movie together or leave books on the topic of S&D lying around. If she asks about it, offer to lend it to her and say it's something that you're turned on by. Show her the Internet sites you've visited. These don't have to be pornographic but are maybe informative and help to answer questions that she or both of you have. If she does make any attempt at being dominant, obey her. If you laugh or demean her attempts it could mean she will never try again. Tell her how lucky you are to have found her and that she is your queen. Build up her confidence and show her she has complete control over you.

You could shop online for some fun sex toys to try out. Make it fun; it doesn't have to be deadly serious. You could start off with a butt plug perhaps which she inserts and orders you to leave in during sex or until she 'has finished with you.' It should be something you both enjoy and when she sees you are enjoying it so much, hopefully she'll want to continue to please you. And in return, you must be willing to do anything she wants that pleases her. Remember, it's not about just one of you getting pleasure, you should both be gaining from this experience or one party is going to want to drop out of it sooner or later. Don't turn your basement into a dungeon after the first conversation because that might just be overkill. In the early stages, plan sessions together always allowing room for her to be creative in her own ways too.

Decide on a safe word. When you're starting out, she might not realize how far is too far. If she is spanking you for example make sure she knows where to spank you which is on the fleshy part of your buttocks and just at the bottom of them. A cane might be a bad idea to start with because they can cause a lot of harm and she is probably not aware of her own strength yet.

Discuss whether you want to flip from one role to another. She might be role-playing at being a domme to please you and even though she might actually enjoy it, she might still prefer being the sub so make sure you take turns if that is what she wants. It's about experimentation and being absolutely clear about what you both want. Being flexible with what you submit to doesn't mean you have to not enjoy it but if you definitely do not wish it to happen make that clear because there can be a fine line between the two.

Communication is the key and you should both decide if male submission is going to be something that you introduce into every sexual session or just now and again. She might want to save it for special occasions to treat you. Talk about whether you would like to involve others and how to do it. You might already know someone or you might choose to visit clubs that have a sexually oriented theme and where you are likely to find other like-minded people.

Some couples enjoy the cuckold scenario when the man has to watch his partner having sex with another man. This might include being tied to a chair beside the bed or even watching a film of it afterwards if it feels more appropriate. This could be combined with punishment afterwards. The man might even have to prepare the woman for sex with the other man by shaving her pubes for instance and applying her nail and toe varnish. He could help her dress tying her into a tight bodice and putting on her stockings. Even brushing her hair would be erotic if they both knew she was being prepared for another man. Of course, this will not be for all couples but can bring some closer together and it's up to you both to decide if this is what you'd like to try. If it does appeal, there are all sorts of ways that you can develop this. For instance the man might have to help getting the man getting undressed on arrival and maybe he could massage him, including giving him a hand job. The man could even be blindfolded during the sex and perhaps allowed to watch a film of it afterwards as a special treat, if he is good that is.

It might be useful if, after every session, you discuss between you what you particularly enjoyed and what did nothing for you. In this way, as you become more experienced between you, she knows what to do to turn you on and those that's she wasting time on. Even the act of talking about it can be quite erotic. You could also engage in phone sex when she tells you what she is going to do to you when you get home. She could say that you are going to be punished for leaving without kissing her that morning and describe in detail what will happen when you get home. Try and take the call in private because it could be very embarrassing to get up from behind your desk at work for instance with a huge erection saying that you have to get home quickly as you run out of the door.

Buy her gifts, including outfits she can wear, and treat her as your superior and make her feel cherished and adored. Most importantly, have fun and lead a fulfilling and sexually exciting life.

Chapter Nine - Role Playing

Now comes the fun part! Literally. No doubt you have your own fantasies to enact but here are some ideas, which, in turn, may give you some new ones. As mentioned previously, the fantasy might remain the same every time or you might choose to vary it and do something entirely different. Things can be spiced up a little by wearing outfits, which can be rented or you can improvise and make your own. And try your best to get into character or you might just end up laughing all the way through it which although it is a lot of fun won't have the desired effect of fulfilling your sexual fantasies.

You might choose to start with something tame and build up so that it gets raunchier as you go along. You might find that you are both exceptionally turned on by the experience or that you move at a different pace, so try and make allowances for each other and adapt to each other's rhythm. As you know, rhythm is especially important when it comes to most sexual acts.

Because you have discussed at length what sort of things you both want to explore, you have already set boundaries so things shouldn't get out of hand. If you do feel unsafe, that is that this is not for you at all, then remember your safe word and say it, loud and clear. The nature of the beast probably demands that you will feel in peril at times, especially if you have set out that corporal punishment will be doled out, that's exactly the name of the game. Right? You are supposed to feel a sense of fear and scary anticipation.

The following examples are just that. They are loose suggestions, which can be varied as, and how you wish - or how your partner wishes. As long she knows what you like, then she can of course take you by surprise and introduce her own ideas, which will probably by more exciting for you both anyway. First of all, take turns to read through the fantasies below and discuss them together saying which ones turn you on even breaking things down and saying why particular aspects of the fantasy excite you. You could take parts from all of them or incorporate just parts of any of them into your own fantasies. Hopefully, this will get you in the mood immediately or you could plan something special for the week-end or whenever you are both free to spend time together uninterrupted and have a good time.

It might be a good idea for your partner to invest in some garments in a sexy material such as leather, PVC, latex or lace, whatever turns you - and her - on. Perhaps you could get some accessories too such as a dog collar and lead. Improvisation can go a long way so have things you can use as ties and blindfolds. You can use leather belts or household objects. Be creative and use your imagination - both of you. I have written these fantasies from the point of view of your partner because she is likely to be in charge most of the time. But this is a chapter you should perhaps share because it is up to your partner to take the lead in these fantasies. In fact, it might be a good idea for you both to share the entire book.

Sex Slave

This is quite a common one so probably a good place to start. Wear your sexiest and most dominant outfit. Leather always goes down well as does stockings and high leather boots. Perhaps you could round this off with crotch less pants or a thong and a basque, which exposes your breasts. If you have a peaked hat that would finish off your outfit nicely. Wear red lipstick and apply makeup that makes your eyes look dramatic. If you don't possess a whip already, use a leather belt instead. Be inventive, it might be a spatula or a fly swat, which would be particularly appropriate to make him feel as demeaned as you can muster. Now you must pick something - anything - that your partner needs punishing for. This might be leaving the bathroom in a mess even after you have told him constantly about it. Without saying anything leave the room and go the place, which you intend to use for his punishment and get into your gear. When you are ready, and have prepared the scene, get him to join you, either by calling him if he is within earshot or call him on his cell phone and tell him where to find you. If he refuses, then show him how angry you are and tell him it is of extreme importance that he comes.

The sight of you in your sexy get-up should make him gasp. Now approach him using your sexiest hip swaying walk and holding a tie behind your back. Go up to him and kiss him deeply. As you do so take hold of his wrists and put them behind his back. Desist kissing him, walk around him and tie his hands behind him. Secure him firmly so he is unable to move to resist you, you could tie him to a chair, which is already set up for him to take a seat. He has to sit and listen to what you intend to do to him. If he tries to escape, slap him.

Now you have to tell him why you have tied him up so you say that you are going to punish him because that seems to be the only thing that will get the message across and through his thick head that he must clean up after himself. Tell him that you are going to cut off his clothes. If he protests, slap him hard across the face again and repeat until he promises to stay quiet. He is to remain completely naked for the whole of your time alone together; hopefully this can be for a whole weekend.

Tell him that after you have meted out some physical punishment, he will then go, at the end of a lead, the end of which you will hang onto, and proceed to clean the bathroom. When it is cleaned to your satisfaction, he will be allowed to undress you and bathe you. When you have laid in a nice bubble bath, he will fetch you Champagne - or the tipple of your choice. He is to stand with his back to the wall and watch you masturbate. When you are finished, he has to help you get out of the bath and dry you off with a warmed towel.

Tell him to clean the bathroom again and then stay there until you call him. You go to the bedroom and dress in your domme gear again and then call him to you. Tell him to bend over the bed just because you want to hurt him again to make sure that he really has got the message. When you have finished, tell him to stand up and you sit on the edge of the bed with your legs open. Tell him that him that he is allowed to suck on one of your breasts and then just when he is starting to enjoy it, tell him to stop. Lie back on the bed with your legs open and instruct him to lick you and make you come. Then turn round and kneel beside the bed and tell him to mount you. When you are satisfied, tell him to go and prepare some food for you and come and tell you when it is ready. Tell him that he will be punished if it is not to your satisfaction.

Keep on in this fashion for the whole of the weekend, using him to do exactly what you want. Make him sleep at the side of the bed and secure him to the bedpost using the lead or the belt. He must sleep completely naked.

Now you are ready to start the process by cutting off his clothes.

Strict Boss

You are the sort of boss who thinks men are useless, very much like your female counterparts, and only employ the token male because the law says that you have to be fair. You treat them with contempt and they have no alternative but to accept your unwritten terms because there is such a shortage of jobs for men and so they have to do their very best to please you. You are dressed in a business suit and from the outside look very proper. You wear very high heels though and silky or fishnet stockings. Your makeup is immaculate and your lips are red. You call your employee into your office for his annual appraisal. You sit behind a desk or table, which should have a clipboard so that you can make notes. The only other chair in the room apart from yours is not around the table. Use a bell or some kind of buzzer to tell him to come into the room. If he does this without knocking, tell him angrily to get out and do it again. Ask him how he has the audacity to be so informal with you.

Explain that he has to stand throughout and that you are going to ask him a number of questions on which you will mark him. If you do not like the answers, there will be consequences. Tell him that you know that he has to do whatever you want or his job is in danger. Ask him if he is still in agreement with that because he did accept it as a condition of his employment with your company. Now start the questions. They should be as out there as you can make them so he has to give answers that you will not accept. Ask him if he has now realized that women are superior. Does he like it here? Does he get on with his colleagues? Ask him if he thinks he should be allowed to stay with the company. What can he do to make sure that you are happy with him? Is he willing to be on call whenever you want him? You can make up your own questions here which will probably be more personally titillating. Every time he gives an answer, note it down and make him wait. At the end of the questions, say you are going to add his marks up and if they fall below 20, he will be below the required scale and have to make up for it immediately. Of course, he fails miserably so you ask him to strip off until he is completely naked. Stand up and go round the desk. If he is not erect, lift his penis up with a pencil and snort. Make a derogatory comment such as, "I see you fall short in that area too." However, it is more likely he will be erect so take a ruler and measure it and then make the same comment before tapping his penis with the ruler. Order him to lock the door or put something against it so that you cannot be disturbed. Tell him to undress you. When he removes your business suit, you should be wearing very sexy underwear, keep your shoes on. Tell him you are going to punish him for his poor work and his stupid answers in his annual appraisal. Tell him that you will not have to monitor him on a much more frequent basis (choose your own) to ensure he is improving, at least in some areas. Tell him to go to the cupboard/drawer and fetch the paddle you use especially for such occasions. Tell him from now he must address you as Mistress. When he brings back the paddle tell him to lean onto the desk and then start whacking him. Hopefully you have enough privacy so that you can make him whelp. When his ass is good and red, tell him to kneel in front of you and thank you for the experience. If he forgets to address you as Mistress, give him some more punishment. Now sit on the edge of the desk with your legs splayed and tell him to crawl over to you. Invite him to show you what else he can do and that it had better make you very happy. When he has made you come, tell him that you haven't quite finished with him. Insert a butt plug into his anus and tell him that he must not remove it for the rest of the day. You will be checking from time to time that it is still there and he must remain naked so that his superior female colleagues are free to do the same. Tell him that he must clean the building to make up for his shortcomings in other areas and that you will call him back later to teach him a lesson that he needs to learn. Allow him water and a small break but watch him eating as if it disgusts you. Throughout the day, call him back into the 'office' and check that his butt plug is still there. If it isn't, give him more punishment. Later, when you are happy that the house is clean, call him back for the lesson. You should have invested in a strap on dildo, which he should watch you putting on. This should be over your sexy underwear or if you prefer just in your stockings. When you have it on, tell him to lean over the desk for his final lesson and after oiling it up start pumping away at him. When he comes, tell him he is disgusting and to go and clean himself up and come back to you. Okay, one last task. He must make you orgasm before he is allowed to finish for the day. Give him strict instructions to do whatever you enjoy most. When you are satisfied, dismiss him but remind him that you will be calling him back at regular intervals to check on his progress. If he doesn't improve, then the punishment is likely to get much, much worse.

Hostage

You have been asked to look after a hostage who is being held for ransom from a rich and powerful family. He has never known any hardships so you are determined that you will teach him a few lessons of your own. Dress in combats if possible and try and wear a mask over your eyes. The only concession to femininity should be the bright red lipstick and the sexy underwear you are wearing underneath. You could start the roleplay by picking him up in some dark alley or car park and putting a bag over his head. Make sure there are no cameras or you'll soon be seeing some blue lights flashing (or we hope you should!). Splash out and buy some handcuffs, which you should snap on him quickly before bundling him in to the back seat of your car. Drive home and get him in the house without anyone seeing. If you have a basement, take him down there, otherwise, maybe you could keep him in the garage. When you have him back, undress him, still with the bag over his head. Laugh at the size of his penis as you grab hold of it roughly and squeeze it hard. Put a belt around his neck and make it tight enough so that he cannot move. An easy way of securing him would be to put one of the holes over a simple hook. Squeeze his balls hard and then explain that he has been brought here until his father pays you $4m. In the meantime, whether or not his father pays up, you intend to have some fun with him and he is going to find out what it is like to be under the complete surrender of a woman. Ask him if he understands and tell him that to start with he is going to receive a beating, which you are going to take great pleasure in administering. If you have a whip use that, otherwise use a belt and start whipping him on the fleshy part of his butt.

Next you could throw a bucket of cold water over him, which should get rid of any erection that might have popped up. Give his balls another squeeze. Tell him that you are going to inspect him and make sure he is clean before you use him for another purpose. Park his butt cheeks and insert your finger and wiggle it around to arouse him. Tell him you are happy that there is nothing there so far and then put in a butt plug. Spank him a bit and ask him if he is going to be a good boy. Tell him you have not gagged him because he is going to need his mouth but that if he tries to call out for help he will suffer beyond imagination. Put some nipple clamps on him to start with and a cock cage if you have one (always be sure to check out the size is appropriate). Take the bag from his head. You could shine a lamp into his eyes so that he is disoriented and blinded by the flash. Let his eyes become accustomed until they fall on you and then slowly start to undress until you are standing there in all your fantastic glory, hopefully brandishing your whip. Tell him that you are going to release him but he must understand that he must fully submit to your wishes. Ask him if he agrees to do so. If no, give him some more punishment. Tell him that he must address you as Mistress (or whatever you prefer of course). Unhook him and tell him to lick your pussy until you tell him to stop.

If he doesn't please you he will receive more punishment. When he has done so, tell him to go and stand back in the original place where he was secured and wait for you there. Remove his cock cage and squeeze his cock. Place the belt over the hook again so that he is standing there naked and vulnerable and tell him you are going to take some photos to send to his father. Take some photos on your phone and send them to someone you both know saying that you are training him. This is about public humiliation too so that when he sees that person, he won't know where to put himself and will be embarrassed about meeting them. Do it with someone he sees frequently but don't put his job in jeopardy please. Perhaps you could send it to one of your girlfriends so that every time you meet up you can both have a good laugh at his expense and make fun of his little penis. If he protests, ask him how he dare and give him some more punishment. Put the bag back on his head and leave him standing there, tied up and naked, for an hour or so.

When you return, tell him that you have received the ransom but before you release him, he has to service you to your satisfaction. Before releasing him, use a vibrator on his ass and tell him that that is the amount of pleasure you want to receive. Withdraw the vibrator before he comes. Bend over and tell him to take you from the back. Allow him to fondle and kiss your breasts and ask him to suck the nipples. Then stop him abruptly and tell him to get on with his job. When you have finished with him, release his wrists and tell him that he is free to leave but he knows you can come for him any time so always be aware that you can bring him back to do this all again.

Readers' Husband

Tell him that you have received a telephone call from a woman saying that she has spotted your husband at the supermarket and she is now having erotic dreams about him. She cannot stop thinking about him and imagining her hands all over him and being able to do what she wants with him. You said that you were not sure you could agree to that but she begged you and finally you agreed to take some erotic photos of him and send them to her. She said she would be willing to pay but you said that at this stage it would be all right for her to receive the photos for free.

If you changed your mind about sex in the future you might have to watch because he does belong to you and that includes his cock. Tell him that she was very grateful and you felt obliged to offer her this because she lives alone and is totally besotted with him. Tell him she asked you to describe his cock and what you get him to do to you and you told her that he was very good at licking pussy and made you come a lot. Tell him that you said that he liked to be spanked and that you have to keep him in control. She had asked if he would agree to the photographs and you told her that he had no choice because he had to do what you told him sexually.

She asked if she could be allowed to come round and take the photos of him herself but that she wouldn't want him to know it was her or he would recognize her when he saw her in the supermarket again. You had agreed that it would probably be all right but that she should wait to see if she wanted to take it further after seeing the photos you were going to send her. Tell him you found it erotic talking to her over the telephone because she was obviously becoming very aroused and you are sure that she had an orgasm because she was moaning and then screamed and that turned you on too. Say that you might consider a threesome or even a lesbian scenario when he has to watch. But not touch.

When he arrives home after work, tell him to strip off completely and you watch him. Lead him to the bathroom if he is not shaved and put him in the shower while you shave him. Lead him back to the bedroom. By this time he should be nice and erect so tell him that you have to have him inside of you before the session starts. Hopefully you should be nice and wet and ready for him by now but if you are not wet enough yet, rub some baby oil on his cock. Tell him to lie down on the bed and climb on top and ride him for all you are worth, satisfying yourself before the rest of the action begins. When you are finished stand up and get your camera ready. Start by taking some pics of his oily cock. If he has tried to come during the sex, stop him by slowing down. You could also slap his face to take his mind off his cock for a minute. You are in control and you want his cock nice and rigid for the photos. It would be great if you can manage to get a pic of his cock going into you.

Spend some time photographing him in various positions. Use your imagination but this could include him kissing your feet or sucking your toes, licking your pussy, sucking your tits. If you have a camera that you can put on a tripod, so much the better because then you can set it up to take pics of you sitting on his face or servicing you from the back.

You can also be inventive by getting him to kneel on all fours and sticking a dildo in his ass. Open the cheeks of his ass and get a good shot of his ass hole and put your finger in it while you massage his balls. Find the place that is very sensitive between his balls and asshole and stroke that too. Don't let him come because you want him to be erect for as long as possible and deferring climax will be torture for him.

After the session, tell him that you have got some fabulous shots and you are going to meet up with Carla tomorrow for coffee to pass them on and make sure she likes them. At the end of the next day tell him that you went to her house and ended up having sex with her because she got so excited and was so absolutely gorgeous you couldn't resist. Tell him that you ended up licking each other's pussies and sucking on each other's tits. You spanked her for being so naughty but you are going back for more because she was so juicy.

Tell him that she loved your photos and begged you to let her have a go on his cock and that you're considering it. You think you might like the idea of a threesome in fact. She is more than willing and asked if she could come and stay for a weekend and that she would agree to be their sex slave. Say that you told it would be better if both she and he were your sex slaves because you like to be in charge. Tell him she agreed to that and if he is a very good boy and does exactly what he is told, you will arrange it. Of course, he will be her sex slave as well and have to do exactly what you both instruct him to do.

You could show him the photos and tell him what she said to each one and that she started putting her hand in her pants at some point and rubbing herself but that you felt so turned on that you bent her over the table and knelt down and licked her pussy till she was screaming. Tell him that it is a new experience for you but one that you intend to repeat regularly and that she begged you to be her mistress and you agreed. Of course, this is role play but perhaps you will be both so turned on that you may want to turn it into the real thing.

Obviously, these are just a few ideas to set you on the path. I'm sure you have many more you want to live out. You will both find your own preferred level of pain and pleasure: you might not want any pain or you might want to experience real pain. It really is up to you.

Chapter Ten – Slice of Life

As much as I like to keep my life personal, there's so much I can teach my readers through my own experience back when I was still new to the FLR world, so I'm going to proceed to give you a gist of how I found out I was a dom, and how it all started for me. My first experience was not fantastic, but my second was what made me positive that I was meant for this life.

For as long as I can remember, I'd always been assertive and confident in my opinions. Growing up, through college, I'd thought my assertiveness was just a sign of confidence and a sense of self-worth. But that was until I met him. Now, for privacy reasons, I'm going to refer to him as Joshua.

It was sophomore year, and he had the prettiest face I'd ever seen. He usually sat in front of me, and I would notice how he would crane his neck toward me, pretending to borrow a pencil from his friend just to shoot me a glance. I was enchanted.

His hazel eyes glistened, and I felt tingling in my chest whenever he smiled at me, and his dimples sunk deeper into his face. I thought five years ago; I probably would have gone up to him, giggled like a dork, and waited until he asked me out. But I had grown up, and I was beginning to understand what I liked: how I liked my men and what I wanted to do with them.

I knew that through porn. When vanilla videos didn't cut it for me, and maledom videos made me uncomfortable, femdom films were this fascinating discovery that made me find my kinks. But I had never done anything like it, and it was only a theory of what I possibly liked.

And that was the thing. When I saw Joshua, I thought he was the perfect man to put the theory to the test. From the moment I laid my eyes on him, I knew he was going to be the first man I'd ever dominated.

He was nervous when I first approached him – nearly dropped his books. It turned me on how clumsy he had seemed. From a distance, he seemed to be the shy type who was going to continue being flustered until I set him straight. With my hand. Or maybe with a whip. I had already fantasized about it all before I said hello. I didn't know what he was into, but he seemed like the type who would let me do what I wanted to him.

And I wasn't wrong.

Of course, I was the one who asked him out. He was surprised by how confident I seemed – a remark which made me smile because it was almost like a code word for dominant. I thought it was a good sign that he could pick up on that. We walked to a local cafe, and I rushed to the door before he pulled it open for me. I didn't look behind me, but I knew the gesture made him smile. We sat down on a table for two, and I dismissed the waiter who came to our table too soon.

"We're still browsing the menu, thanks," I said, speaking on behalf of Joshua, as well.

I remember the way Joshua looked up at me with his toothy smile, his round cheeks pressing on his eyes as he squinted a little. My eyes were fixed on the menu, but I could see him looking at me. My legs were crossed, and my face was straight as I chewed my gum.

"You're kind of a badass," he commented in almost a murmur.

At this point, it felt like a cue for me to understand him more. I was intrigued, turned on, and almost star-struck.

"I bet you're equally as badass in bed," he continued with a smirk dawning on his face.

Until he said that.

Even though I'd been thinking of nothing but how I'd annihilate him in the bedroom, I didn't like how quickly he sexualized our encounter. I knew he was attracted to me from the way he subtly eyed me, scanning my body up and down and pausing at my bulging tits. But how quickly he had presumed that my approach was sexual turned me off. It was the kind of audacity that I never liked in a man. I liked them shy and reserved, leaving me the space to make the first move. But I didn't want to be picky, so I shrugged it off.

Fast-forward to when our food came, I was already bored out of my mind.

It had been fifteen minutes, and he wouldn't stop talking about himself. He would sometimes let me comment, only to stop me and continue speaking his mind. The worst part was, he couldn't tell how cocky he was being. But aside from his unimpressive personality and juvenile intellect, that wasn't what bothered me. I felt like he had stolen control from me.

But he was a beginner, I was sure. I thought I could still train him. Clearly, he was sexually attracted to me strongly enough to go with the flow, and I still wanted to dominate him.

I asked for the check, and he didn't bother reaching for it. I didn't like that, either. It was almost like he was selectively submissive when it suited him, but still, I shrugged the second red flag off. I smiled at the waiter, my eyes following him until he left.

As soon as he did, I turned to Joshua and said, "So, are we doing this or what?"

He chuckled, almost choking on his own spit. "You mean, like," he paused, lowering his voice, "sex?"

"Clearly," I nonchalantly said, crossing my arms. "Since we both know why we're here, skipping class, we might as well just go for it."

"Fuck, that would be amazing," he said, his eyes growing wide like he had been waiting for me to say that.

Little did I know, this was not going to be a one night stand, but a brief two-month relationship that felt a lot longer because Joshua, as I later found it, knew little about boundaries and personal space.

That afternoon, we walked back to my studio apartment. I kicked the door shut and smiled at him. He smiled back, blushing and glancing at the ground. I was really attracted to him at that moment. It was almost as though I only liked him when he revealed the shy and dorky side of him. I began undressing him, and he was about to undress me.

This was my chance to test it out.

"Don't touch me without permission," I ordered him with a straight face.

For a moment, he was confused. But as I continued to undo his belt, he smiled and understood where this was going.

"This is like, one of my biggest fantasies," he moaned as I pulled his pants down and began caressing his balls. "Fuck," he exclaimed in a whisper.

From the way it started out, I had thought this was going to go smoothly. But then he made those remarks that completely turned me off. As I stripped him naked, grabbed him by the chin, and looked him in the eye while I jerked him off, he said, "Yeah, you like that?" referring to his cock.

I wanted to roll my eyes. He wasn't doing this right. He was too cocky, and it confused me more than anything. I was certainly attracted to him. I found myself smiling as I traced my fingers along the contours of his body, but the moment I looked him in the eye and saw how he smirked, it threw me off. He was a good looking man, but he knew that all too well, and it made it difficult for me to get in the mood.

But there I was. I had stripped a man naked and was leading him to my humble bedroom. When I turned around, I saw how he was checking out the place and nodding. He said he liked my lampshade and smiled. I hated that. He was opting out of our little power-play while we were in the midst of it. This guy clearly had no idea how to please a dominant woman.

I raised a finger to his lips. "Shut up," I said, trying to make it sound kinky as much as I could, but I really was annoyed with him.

He smirked again, seating himself on my bed as he licked his lips.

As I stood before him, glancing at his already hard cock, I kept thinking of how forced this felt. I didn't like how he treated it like a game. It wasn't a game to me; it was how sex should be. Surely, I knew that men were not really my servants, but I didn't like how Joshua reminded me of that by opting out of the dynamic every now and again.

I would have described him as someone who was too demanding, but I later discovered that he was needy, as well.

There he was, still on my bed. He looked up at me and pointed to his cock. "You can use teeth if you want. I like a little pain in that area."

You're not supposed to tell me that, Joshua, I thought to myself.

I was almost wet a couple of minutes ago, but now I was dry as a desert. I gave him a few spanks, and he smiled and giggled every time my hand landed on his round ass cheeks. I guess he really was submissive, but not the kind I liked. He didn't take it as seriously as I would have wanted him to. And I guess I also took him by surprise when I revealed I was a dom.

We didn't have sex that night. I didn't want to. He was disappointed, but he didn't say anything. He asked me to stay over, and I gave him no straight answer. He did anyway, and I later found myself caught in a relationship I never asked for. He noticed I wasn't happy with the way he presented himself to me, and he began to change.

But instead of changing into my type, he changed into this excessively needy idiot who would follow me around the apartment with nothing on but boxer briefs. He would sometimes purposely piss me off, thinking it would get him another spanking. Ironically, the last time he got on my nerves, it earned him a break-up. I asked him to leave, and he never stopped texting me since. He still does sometimes, and I cringe every time I remember putting up with him.

Joshua made me question everything. I wondered whether the lifestyle I wanted was even real, or if it were just something idealistic that we only get to see in porn. I thought that perhaps my tendencies were best left in my fantasies, which I would maybe one day express through literature in an attempt to normalize FLR. Because, surely, if I could only see myself as a dom in any relationship, there must have been women out there who felt the same way. I just wasn't sure whether there would be enough men in the world who would mutually want such a relationship.

I wasn't exactly devastated, but I was definitely irked, and the feeling lingered for a few months until it slowly faded. It didn't dissipate, though. I always felt like there was something missing from my life, something that was never really going to be fulfilled because it was nothing but a fantasy inspired by adult films.

But that was until I met Brandon.

I didn't think much of him when I first met him. He was about the same height as me, but I always wore heels, so it felt like I towered over him whenever we talked. It was back in the corporate days when I worked next to him in a cubicle at a PR company. He would always try to find an excuse to speak to me, and I played along.

It was a few months until he seemed interested in me as more than just a colleague. I liked how he never flirted with me and only gave me the opportunity to initiate flirts. He was a funny guy and always made jokes about how I could easily destroy him if I wanted to. He was probably right, but I wasn't sure whether we thought of the same scenario.

I would catch him looking at me quite often, but he would always smile and look away. He rarely ever looked me in the eye for too long, especially while we made conversation. I liked how shy he was, and I eventually asked him out.

Brandon seemed surprised, but he never acted like too much of a dork. He was a shy gentleman who was as eloquent as he was kind. We were initially going to head to a nice cozy restaurant, but it was closed for renovations that night.

"Wanna get some corn dogs and take a walk?" he suggested, gesturing to the corn dog stand with his chin. He had his hands tucked into his pockets whenever he was around me. It was a little chilly at the time, but I knew that wasn't why he hid his hands.

I noticed how they shook a little whenever I was physically close to him. He was definitely attracted to me, and I was quickly growing to feel the same way.

I took the offer, and we went to get snacks. That day, I wore high-heeled boots, and whenever we were about to step down the sidewalk, he would link his arm with mine and help me down. I didn't need help, but I liked the gesture. Although he was shy, and I felt in control, he was still a gentleman that made sure I was comfortable.

It was always the little details that I paid attention to, like how he acted when we stopped by for ice-cream. The number of men that have said something along the lines of, "And perhaps a strawberry ice-cream cone for the lady?" made me think that men were just programmed to think that women liked everything pink and sweet. The only shade of pink I liked was a hand-print on a man's ass. And I guess Brandon, deep down, knew that.

He gave me the space to speak for myself and always listened when we conversed. Even though there was a back-and-forth, I still felt like I was the one leading it, and I didn't have to force it, either. That night, he walked me home and said goodnight. He stood there for a moment, almost slowly turning around to leave, hoping that it wouldn't be the end of it. I pulled him close and sucked a kiss out of his plump lips. I could feel him smiling on my lips. The kiss was slow and sensual, and he kept his hands to himself.

When I slowly pulled away, his face was flushed, and he kept combing his hair back with his fingers, flustered, and a little giggly.

"I think you just might be one of the most intimidating women I've ever met," he said, smiling. "I think it's my weakness."

That was it. I knew things would work out between us the moment he said that. He was the perfect blend of gentlemen and sub, and as much as I didn't want to rush things between us, I couldn't wait to have him in my bed.

Brandon was the one who taught me how FLR relationships should go. I'd previously thought that I had to make myself assertive in order to advertise myself as a dominant woman, but that was just the vulgar way to do it, and it attracted the wrong men. I later learned that you know a man is submissive when he gives you the space to make the first moves, while also very subtly expressing interest. They may initiate a conversation with you, but they rarely ever come forward with their feelings for you unless you allow them to. It all just comes naturally.

I had mistakenly thought that men had to be trained and informed of my ways, but I realized that I skipped quite a few essential steps. I was thinking with a sexual mindset, and that always ended up landing me creeps. There's more to an FLR than sex. Dominant women generally lead in the relationship, while also giving their partners the space to make decisions for themselves. This wasn't something that you sat down and announced to a man on a first date, but it was definitely something that you picked up on the more you socialized.

It was three dates later with Brandon until I invited him home. During these couple of weeks, we texted and face-timed. A lot. We talked about everything that we liked in more detail. That was when I realized that you should never surprise a man by the fact that you're a dominant woman. I thought I'd have to invite them over and surprise them with a whip, hoping they would be into that kind of thing. But that never turned out the way I wanted it to. Even when they were into it, it would all seem too forced, like it was an act on display.

That's why I brought it up to Brandon. We were exchanging provocative photos one day, and I straight up asked him if he would be interested in an FLR power-play in bed. He replied with, "You fucking bet," which was the fastest text he'd ever sent me, and it made me chuckle. He immediately confirmed that he was pursuing a mistress, but that he was also looking for a serious relationship. Just like me, Brandon was seeking a full-blown FLR. It seemed too good to be true, but there it was.

We agreed to meet that weekend, and we treated ourselves to steak and wine at a nearby restaurant. After he'd walked me home, I asked him if he wanted to stay over with me that night. His big brown eyes widened, and he immediately stuffed his hands in his pockets and swayed a little as he glanced at my front door. He nodded, then said yes.

I knew he was nervous. He knew exactly what was going to happen.

As I led him to the living room, I felt his eyes caressing me from behind, and he unsurprisingly looked away as soon as I turned around.

"You can sit down, you know," I said with a smile, looking up at him after he'd been standing over the sofa for a full minute, scanning my body with a shy smile.

He nodded and sat on the two-seater sofa with his hands on his lap. "So," he said, stifling a chuckle. "I'm sorry," he laughed. "I know you probably can't tell, but I'm just a little bit nervous."

I liked the way he sometimes mocked his own shyness, thinking it would turn me off. But it had the opposite effect on me.

"I like that you are," I replied, scooching closer to him.

He didn't look my way, but he smiled as he noticed I was almost close enough for my bare thighs to touch his.

Brandon's smile grew wider. "Do you like it when men are completely shaky leaves around you?"

I playfully rolled my eyes. "Sometimes. Let's just say I don't get along well with cocky men."

"I see," he nodded.

"Or generally dominant men," I clarified, reminding him of our conversation.

"That's comforting. I'm the complete opposite of all these qualities," he chuckled. "At least, that's what I recently realized, and it's probably why I haven't been dating as much," he said briskly, shaking his head as he spoke. He was still a little nervous, but he was getting used to being around me.

I put my arm on the backrest and played with his hair as he spoke. He paused for a moment, then continued, "But I feel more comfortable around you. I feel like women, in general, tend to expect me to get take care of everything for them," he paused, "Not that there's anything wrong with that, I'm just not that kind of guy, I guess."

I stifled a grimace. I remember how successful I felt at that moment like I had finally found the perfect guy for me. Still, I had no clue how rough I could be with him in bed, but even if I had to go easy on him, the man was worth it.

Brandon craned his neck toward me and glanced at my lips, squinting his eyes ever-so-slightly as if cueing for me to kiss him. I immediately leaned toward him, sucking on his bottom lip. He took in a deep breath and was smiling as I kissed him.

But he still kept his hands to himself.

I slid my hand to his lap, grabbing his hands and sliding them to my breasts. My eyes were closed, but I could feel him squirming a little. It was almost as though I could feel his heart beating. He was about to unbutton my blouse. U pulled back and slapped his hand.

"Did I grant you permission to do that?" I playfully snarled.

His chest was heaving. The more I got into character, the more it seemed to excite him.

"Sorry, mistress," he whispered. Finally, hearing someone call me that was like music to my ears.

Admittedly, I was becoming more impatient, and I immediately stripped him down. I hadn't even touched his cock yet, and he was rock hard. I loved how he knew that his hands had to be kept to himself unless I otherwise gave him permission to touch me.

It was kinky and sensual. It was the only sex I've ever had that felt real. I had been beginning to think that I was just not into sex since all it did was disappoint me. But with Brandon, with someone who allowed me to dominate him and actually enjoyed it, sex was captivating.

It was a night full of teasing, spanking, and fun punishments. He was also serious in his character, and he knew exactly what we were doing. That made it feel natural and spontaneous. It was exactly what I needed.

He stayed over that night, and we didn't stop talking since. We eventually dated, and power-play dominated (pun definitely intended) our everyday lives. He had quit his job at the PR company we worked at, and began working from home. He would let me know before I came home whether he was done with his projects. Whenever he had any tight deadlines, I would come back, order takeout, and we'd just watch some television before going to bed.

But on the nights both of us had the time, we would communicate via text beforehand, and it made it much easier and more natural for me to come home, not as Alexandra, but as Mistress. Sometimes, the power-play would start before I got home, too. I would order him to send me photos of himself in some poses, and he would abide. When I finally got home, that's when I'd decide whether I wanted to reward or punish him that night. He was always happy to get a face-sitting punishment, and his reward was either a blowjob or being allowed to penetrate me.

Our relationship was constantly evolving, and we always tried new things. Sometimes, he wouldn't like our new games, but he would go crazy about others. He was always open with me about what he was comfortable with; I was the same way. We never ventured with trying anything new in bed before discussing it beforehand.

If there was a formula for making this relationship successful, it was probably that period before we had sex, where we talked about everything we liked before giving it a try. Our first couple of times were magical, and the rest were full of experimentation and excitement. I thought I'd have to reveal the dominatrix that I am to men once we were in bed, but it turned out to be the least practical method I'd ever tried. I guess you could say I've learned that the hard way, and now I always talk to my partners before we decide to try out our roles, to see if both of us would be comfortable with it.

Conclusion

I hope you have enjoyed the book and that it has given you some ideas and helped you feel as if you are on an exciting journey to self-discovery and sexual fulfillment. It can feel lonely out there when you are just starting to explore the unknown territory and you feel like you're the only person on Earth that feels the way you do. This is amplified by the fact that dominant women are hard to find and men wishing to be dominated far outnumber them. But this goes to prove that it is a more common sexual proclivity than we might have initially thought.

I hope that you now feel optimistic about being a male submissive and that you have taken away new ideas of how to introduce this into your life. Now you know where to look for someone or how to introduce it to your current partner. Rarely does it exist in someone's life in entirety. In fact, I imagine that would be nigh on impossible but only you will know to what degree you can allow it into yours - or to what degree you wish to have it in your life.

I hope that the most important messages I have conveyed are that you are not alone, there is a growing number of men who are feeling more comfortable about admitting that they feel like this. You should also be confident about introducing the concept to an existing partner now too and fully appreciate how important discussion is within that relationship. It doesn't have to be the dominant factor in your life or your sex life and it's about finding a level that you are both comfortable and happy with. Your partner might only know how you feel if you tell her; she's not a mind reader. Even if the idea is totally taboo to her at first, give her time and show her ways that you can start with a light touch. Start treating her like a queen, buy her gifts, and surprise her with a sexy massage. Take your time to please her sexually and in day to day life. I guarantee that pretty soon she'll start appreciating all the extra attention and want to please you too.

All too often, people keep their thoughts and desires to themselves because they think that they're a bit off the wall or feel embarrassed or even ashamed of how they feel. If you can identify that this was you in the past, now you have the ammunition to get what you want for the future. Hopefully, this book has helped in your self-exploration and made you feel that it is quite normal to have these desires. In fact, I want to stress again, that as long as you are not hurting anyone, what you do in private is totally your own business and no one else's. Depriving yourself of things you want pleases no one so what is the point? You should live your life to the full and that should encompass your sex life too so don't be afraid to go out and get what you want.

I wish you well on your journey and hope you find fulfillment. In all areas of your life!

Before You Go

Please leave and honest Amazon review and don't forget to visit my site alexandramorris.com

Check out my other books:

Dominant Women

Erotic Hypnosis

Kink 101

Introduction to the submissive lifestyle

CPSIA information can be obtained
at www.ICGtesting.com
Printed in the USA
BVHW050933290323
661354BV00013B/468

9 789198 604757